Infinite War

Faces of the New Global Conflict

Infinite War
Faces of the New Global Conflict

Compiled by
Hugo Achá

Hugo Achá / David E. Spencer / Leonardo Coutinho
Juan Antonio Blanco / Maibort Petit / Carlos Sánchez Berzain

FOUNDATION FOR
HUMAN RIGHTS
IN CUBA

Published by Foundation for Human Rights in Cuba
Miami, Florida
www.fhrcuba.org

Compiled by Hugo Achá
Assistant Researcher, Mariana Suarez

November 2019

ISBN-13: 978-1-7339274-2-0

Table of Contents

Preface

With this compilation of essays, the Foundation for Human Rights in Cuba (FHRC) wishes to encourage the study of a new type of global conflict faced by open societies. From the Cold War between ideological blocs we have moved onto a new conflict between open, democratic, rule-of-law abiding societies, and on the other hand a fluid coalition of States and dissimilar irregular forces that represent various forms of transnational organized crime.

Part of these actors had already developed since the Cold War era a kind of multiform conflict against Western countries. **The Cold War is over, but not this global conflict: an infinite war to which they have no intention of putting an end through negotiations.** It involves States as different as Russia and China, Syria and Venezuela, Cuba and North Korea, Bolivia and Iran. Also, irregular narco terrorist groups, such as Hezbollah, FARC, ELN and others, are part of that anti-Western alliance.

The persistence of the false criterion that some of these societies are governed today by leftist governments conceals the criminal essence of the oligarchies that hold real power and that have appropriated their respective States for their own benefit.

We are not in the presence of leftist or "revolutionary" processes, but in the face of the emergence of a regional criminal alliance under the guise of the so-called "Socialism of the 21st Century." A new type of State, criminal and transnational, linked to drug trafficking and terrorism, has established itself under the noses of an inter-American system that does not know how to classify what is now confronting it, and for that reason fails to assess the seriousness of the threat it represents for its national security or is incapable of finding effective ways to deal with it. The merger of the criminal oligarchies in two countries crowned that process and produced a mutation, a new species: **Cubazuela, the first Latin American transnational criminal State**, which brings together and coordinates its regional and extra-regional peers, from Bolivia to Iran along with irregular narco terrorist forces from the Middle East and Latin America.

The same is true for the subversive strategy and methodology of the new transnational criminal alliance. It is not possible to stop it if one does not understand the way in which these States, guided by Havana, carry out a multiform, asymmetric, total and endless war. This new form of conflict employs military and intelligence resources, as Hugo Achá warns in his paper on the **Infinite War**, but also relies on rigorous plans of influence on cultural, academic, informational and other civil society movements and institutions.

Traditional doctrines of international relations cannot fully capture the implications of that fact. And as long as the magnitude of what has happened, and its consequences, is not understood, it will not be possible to design the lines of action that need to be taken to contain and reverse that monstrosity.

The transition we are witnessing today in some former communist societies is not from totalitarian to liberal states as Francis Fukuyama in the1990's, but that of communism to mafia states.

The value of this collection of essays is that its point of departure is the recognition that we are facing a new species, a dangerous mutation of communism into criminal States, which today are developing a new paradigm of global conflict.

The authors share this concern and seek ideas to remedy it, although each author is responsible for their own arguments and conclusions.

Foundation for Human Rights in Cuba

Infinite War
From the People's War to the Infinite War.
Conflict as an End in Itself

Hugo Achá

Hugo Antonio Achá is the Director of Research and Out-
reach for the Foundation for Human Rights in Cuba
(FHRC). He is also an International Fellow for the Center
for a Secure Free Society (SFS).

Mr. Achá got his Law Degree from the Universidad Mayor
de San Simon in Cochabamba-Bolivia in 1995, his post-
graduate education include courses and diplomas in the
Netherlands (Maastricht School of Management) and Brazil (Universidade Federal de Minas Gerais) and a Master's
Degree in Security, Defense and Development (Escuela de
Altos Estudios Nacionales de la Universidad Militar de Bolivia). He is also an alumnus of the William J. Perry Center
for Hemispheric Defense Studies in Washington DC.

Mr. Achá is a recognized researcher and lecturer in Counterterrorism and Combating Transnational Organized
Crime and a guest lecturer to different academic institutions
as well as an analyst for several media outlets both in the
US and Latin America.

Summary

The appearance of a hybrid entity that is a combination of a political and a criminal organization has brought about the emergence
of a new type of war. The seizure of power by this organization
and its control over a formal State presents us with a new way of
waging war.

A war thus conceived no longer has a time frame, with a beginning
of hostilities or a formal end. Its goal is not only to obtain victory,

nor are its methods limited to the classical concepts of war, be it the traditional meaning or its asymmetric development. This war is total, social and permanent; all areas of society are considered theaters of operations; and the illicit underworld, understood as part of society, is the most efficient logistical provider and the most convenient generator of conflicts.

This new type of war sees in conflict its justification, and in the use of absolutely all forms of struggle the way to permanently achieve its dominance and its victory.

Introduction

The analysis of conflict, its nature and its evolution, has almost always suffered from two major problems.

First, only the most obvious manifestations of conflict are analyzed; which means an interpretation based on essentially the wrong parameters; the wars of the future are interpreted through the concepts of the last war. Second, the wars are analyzed through the prism of our own principles and values, thus creating a mirror image effect.

The current approach tries to avoid these limitations, analyzing it from an open perspective, understanding conflict as all-encompassing or total activity, an approach which only two radical ideologies have taken it in the history of mankind.

National Socialism with its Total War concept, and Marxism Leninism with its Absolute War concept, both strangely similar in proclaiming that all methods are valid for obtaining victory; as well as that all forms of struggle must be employed, since the victory of the "revolution" justifies such an extreme, and once victory is achieved, a "better" world awaits the revolutionary.

In that regard, Marxism-Leninism achieved much greater advances in the development of theory and doctrine, not only because of the theory developed by such historic figures such as Mao Tse Tung, but because a careful reading of the postulates and analysis developed by Lenin indicate many things that even many Communist militants have forgotten..

Marxism Leninism created concepts that from their very beginning demonstrated a more universal vision while avoiding distractions. These concepts — such as the People's War, the Popular War, and the War of Liberation — are merely different stages of an evolution whose essence has not changed, but whose operational and strategic capabilities have long ago left behind even the constraints generated by the same ideology that conceived them.

Thus, it is essential to understand that, as Marks and Rich clearly point out:

> "There is a key point that is evident in relation to the issue of the People's War. Far from being an anachronism, much less a mere bag of techniques, the people's war always raises a concept that has been in military history since the beginning of time: guerrilla warfare, and merges it symbiotically with another concept which has also been present since time immemorial in politics: the rebellion and its effort to obtain power." [1]

This concept nullifies the limitations that the conception of war suffers in Western society, for there are no ethical limits ideological or moral constraints: the goal is victory and once again we turn to Marks and Rich to define this approach:

> "Victory ensures obtaining power, which in turn is essential to keep a population under the domination of a new political order."[2]

---

[1] Marks, Thomas & Rich, Paul. (2017). "Back to the future – people's war in the 21st century". *Small Wars & Insurgencies*. Vol 28. No. 3, 409-425.

[2] Ibid.

Once this is understood, it is easier to realize how People's War or Popular War has been employed to develop a new concept in which victory is no longer framed in ideological terms.

A War thus conceived no longer has a discreet timeline, a beginning of hostilities or a formal end. Its goal is not to just achieve a formal victory. Its methods are not limited to the classical concepts of war, or traditional theory of asymmetric war. The new war is total, covers all areas of society, is permanent, and occurs in all theaters of operations. One of the most important areas is the illicit underworld — mainly drug trafficking and corruption — as it is the most efficient source of logistics, and the most convenient generator of conflicts. Conflict is its own justification in this new type of war, and the use of absolutely all forms of struggle as the path to permanently achieve domination and victory.

How did we get here?

The evolution towards this type of war has not been a linear progression, although landmark cases can be clearly identified, including notably those of Cuba, Bolivia, Russia, China and Venezuela, as well as those of the FARC and Hezbollah.

Cuba in Context

To understand this approach, it is necessary to realize the strategic concepts developed by the Cuban regime since its inception.

Shortly after the triumph of the revolution that overthrew Fulgencio Batista, Fidel Castro said that the conflict was only beginning, and that the real enemy was the United States of America. This idea and the clear and unequivocal objective identified by Fidel Castro in his capacity as Prime Minister of the revolutionary Government and Secretary of the PURSC (United Party of the Socialist Revolution, in Spanish), are contained in a speech delivered at the conclusion of a series of meetings with the Cuban intellectuals at the National Library between June 16th and June 30th 1961, where the following statement stand out:

> "We believe that the revolution still has many battles to fight, and we believe that our first thought and our first concern must be what is to be done so that the revolution comes out victorious. Because that is the first thing, first is the revolution itself. And then, only then, we'll worry about the other issues."[3]

This postulate has usually been overshadowed by the maxim pronounced at the same event and then repeated on March 13, 1966, on the steps of the University of Havana: "Within the Revolution everything, outside the Revolution nothing." This more widely disseminated and popular phrase deliberately ignores the deeper content of the first quote. This stems from the Leninist concept that morality, legality, and the most elementary principles are subsumed by the higher moral imperative of the triumph of a revolution, which is basically nothing less than the perpetuation of an authoritarian and caustic personalist regime, whose survival must prevail over any other consideration.

In that context, this concept is nothing less than a variant of the Communist Morality as defined by Lenin in his speech at the First Session of the Third Congress of the Communist Youth of Russia, in Moscow, on October 2nd, 1920.

> "In what sense do we deny morals and ethics? We deny them in the sense that the bourgeoisie has proclaimed them, deducting them from the commandments." To add a little further, "Our morality is entirely subordinated to the interests of the class struggle of the proletariat. Our ethics has

---

[3] Speech delivered by Commander Fidel Castro Ruz, Prime Minister of the Revolutionary Government and Secretary of the PURSC in his speech delivered at the conclusion of the Meetings with the Cuban Intellectuals, held at the National Library on June 16th, 23rd and 30th, 1961.

as starting point the interests of the class struggle of the proletariat."[4]

With an understanding of the underlying morality, it is easy to understand the military doctrine of the Cuban State, which postulates "The military doctrine of the Cuban State is the set of ideas and definitions scientifically based, adopted on the essence, the objectives, the character, peculiarities and consequences of war; the preparation of the country to wage it successfully; and the methods for its realization and conduct, in order to face a military aggression."[5]

The "peculiarities" as well as that hypothetical "aggression" can only be understood through the Marxist-Leninist lens. Every action, absolutely everything, is justified in the context of the so-called "War of the Whole People" to defend the revolution both inside and outside Cuban territory, and any event that is deemed as an "aggression" against the revolution — meaning, the regime — is a casus belli even in the event that the "enemy" is not even remotely aware that their actions are considered such.

The Transition to the "War of Liberation" and the Illicit Underworld as a Resource

The evolution of this concept was by no means exclusively Cuban, and its discussion, implementation, and justification are found throughout the world in the field of insurgencies and Irregular Warfare.

---

[4] V.I. Lenin. *Tasks of the Communist Youth*, Speech at the First Session of the Third Congress of the Communist Youth of Russia in Moscow, on October 2nd, 1920.

[5] Cuban Military Doctrine.

Among the relevant works are those of Truong Nhu Tang[6] who clearly describe how the use of criminal networks, such as drug trafficking, were essential to the Viet Minh in its operations against the French in Indochina, as well as a major source of funding for the National Liberation Front, better known as the Viet Cong, and the Khmer Rouge, during the Vietnam War.

Innumerable variants occurred throughout the Cold War, but the central conclusions of the analysis conducted by the Soviet intelligence services made it absolutely clear that solid finances were essential. Without it, the defeat of the West and more specifically of the United States was unthinkable, given the American socioeconomic characteristics and means of production.

Therefore, beginning in 1954 the aforementioned intelligence services made a change to Soviet doctrine in order to reduce the financial and logistical advantage of the United States. This process, addressed by the government of Nikita Khrushchev, can be summarized as follows:

> The "Revolutionary War" was set aside as an isolated concept, and integrated into the operations now referred to as "Wars of Liberation."

This designation diversified the options, multiplied the foci of conflict and avoided the apparent connection between the "internationalist" status of these initiatives and their aggressive nature, making them appear as efforts of "liberation" or of fighting against "imperialist colonialism."

---

[6] Truong Nhu Tang. *A Vietcong Memoir: An inside Account of the Vietnam War and Its Aftermath,* New York: Vintage Books, 1986.

The Underworld as an Axis

From the Soviet Union to Putin's Russia

To make these initiatives viable, three strategic lines were adopted:

1. Sustained international drug trafficking operations.
2. Sustained operations of transnational organized crime.
3. Sustained operations of international terrorism.

These lines of effort were to impact the following areas:

1. Weaken the enemy society (meaning the US.)
2. Corrupt the political, institutional and financial system of the enemy.
3. Destabilize States close to the United States, thus creating the conditions for a "War of Liberation."

The operational responsibility of the terrorism and drug lines of action fell to the director of Soviet military intelligence (GRU) and the Organized Crime line, with special emphasis on money and asset laundering, fell to the State Security Committee (KGB).[7]

A documented description of these activities can be found in various documentary sources, but it is especially well described by Robert Grossman and Christoper Story[8] as well as in the work by William R. Corson and Robert T Crowley.[9]

Concurrent tools to facilitate these strategic lines included the participation of allied intelligence services, predominantly the Intelligence and Counterintelligence Services of Cuba (MININT,

---

[7] "Drugs, Russia And Terrorism, Part 1". Published by *Newsmax*, March 7, 2002

[8] Joseph D. Douglass, *Red Cocaine: The Drugging of America and the West*, Edward Harle, 1999

[9] William R. Corson and Robert T. Crowley. *The New KGB: Engine of Soviet Power*, New York: Morrow, 1985

DI, G2), Czechoslovakia (StB) and the German Democratic Republic (Stasi), as well as the creation of operating platforms such as the Tricontinental.

This, however, should not lead us to ignore the role that these lines played and continue to play in the geostrategic design of Vladimir Putin's Russia, as described by Galeotti:

> "The Russian State is highly criminalized, and the interrelation between the criminal "underworld" and the political "supra world" has led the Russian government to use criminals as instruments of political action."[10]

Furthermore:

> "Russian criminal organizations in Europe have been used for various purposes, including as sources of financial resources for complex operations (Black Cash), for the launch of cyber-attacks, as platforms for action and political influence, to traffic goods and services, and even to carry out selective killings under the Kremlin's orders."[11]

Cocaine Makes an Entrance

An event that has remained in the dark for a long time depicts the absolute pragmatism of this way of conceiving war.

The Cuban intelligence services noted with growing concern in the late 1970s that the alliance with the Soviet Union had increasingly difficulties to financially support the island country, and even though operations along the lines oriented by Moscow had already been developed, it was the cocaine explosion and its sustained demand which opened the doors to a new chapter in the development

---

[10] Mark Galeotti. "Crimintern: How the Kremlin Uses Russia's Criminal Networks in Europe", European Council on Foreign Relations, 18th April 2017.

[11] Ibid.

of the concept of the People's War, moving towards its current form of the War understood as the Social and Endless War.

This event was the Castro-Suarez Alliance; that is, the agreement between Fidel Castro and the Bolivian drug lord Roberto Suárez. This agreement merits further examination.

Roberto Suárez, known at the time as the King of Cocaine, established a true drug empire by developing atypical operational tenets for his operations. His "Corporation" developed its activities differently from the criminal organizations of his time and the effects of its conceptual evolution are still clearly felt today.

The Corporation did not carry out its operations in one-dimension; in addition to the business, it was deeply involved in the solution of the social needs of its population base.

Violence was not exercised indiscriminately but rather selectively and focused. A coercion and intimidation apparatus of quasi-military characteristics was organized, but its use was more dissuasive than offensive.

The finances generated were used, together with the licit activities, to spread the benefits and launder the capital on an unprecedented scale. Legitimate operations (real estate investments, front companies, bank transactions, etc.), albeit fueled by the flow of illegal proceeds, allowed the Corporation to build an economic network that transcended not only the country of origin of its illegal activity but also the whole hemisphere region, even reaching into Europe.

Finally, the penetration of the political establishment was deliberate and planned, developing political discourse justifying the business. With this discourse they were able to penetrate several political parties and movements notwithstanding their ideological position.

The Connection

The attempts by the Cuban regime to approach the Corporation were put into practice through the M-19 and Carlos Lehder, and the official in charge was the then Cuban ambassador to Bogotá, Fernando Ravelo.

> "In January 1983, Roberto and Escobar (Pablo Escobar) finally agreed to meet in Bogota with the representative of the Cuban government. Ravelo received them at the embassy accompanied by the head of the MC Department (Convertible Currency, in Spanish), under the Ministry of Interior, Colonel Antonio de la Guardia, who transmitted the invitation of General Arnaldo Ochoa to visit Cuba."[12]

The diagnosis made by Pablo Escobar summarizes and portrays the Cuban situation while demonstrating the operational agility of transnational crime organizations and their opportunistic and highly effective essence:

> "Department MC, Marijuana-Cocaine? We have them where we wanted, my boss. These Cubans are begging for silver. The alms they receive from the Russians are less and less. They are being drip fed."[13]

The sources contain detailed elements and a level of knowledge of the highest circles of the Cuban military and political leadership that are surprising even today:

> "At the Varadero airport they were given a VIP reception by Rene Rodríguez, president of the Cuban Institute of Friendship with the Peoples (ICAP, in Spanish) and Admiral Aldo Santamaria, military commander of the Cuban

---

[12] Aida Levy. *El Rey de la Cocaína: Mi vida con Roberto Suarez y el nacimiento del primer narcoestado*, United States:Vintage, 2013

[13] Ibid.

navy. During the trip to the Naval Operations Command, Rodríguez and Santamaría told them about the high interest Fidel and his surroundings had in using drug trafficking as a weapon against US imperialism, and supporting Colombian guerrilla groups, especially those of the M-19, with funds from the traffic."[14]

The description of the operational coordination meeting to finalize the details of the agreement with the participation of General Ochoa and Minister José Abrantes is higly interesting because of its financial scope and strategic projection.

However, that is not the end of it. The sources clearly reveal Fidel Castro's position on the issue, as well as Raúl Castro's participation:

"At the Havana airport they boarded a Mi-24 (Sic) helicopter that flew them to the island of Cayo Piedra. When they flew over the paradisiacal property, they were dazzled by the magnificence of the construction. They landed at the helipad, where they were received by the Minister of Defense. "Welcome, gentlemen! My brother is waiting for you upstairs," said Raúl Castro, who led them in the midst of strong surveillance by dozens of civil guards and military snipers to the main hall of the mansion.

Next, Fidel Castro spoke:

"Thank you for finally accepting Ochoa's invitation. You will be the missile with which I will break the blockade and the unjust embargo that my country suffers."[15]

In summary, Suarez understood the Corporation as an organization without borders, endowed with the ability to generate unlimited economic resources. He developed it beyond a mere criminal gang.

---

[14] Ibid.

[15] Ibid.

He gave it transnational characteristics, made it operate financially on a global scale, structured the cartels as operational divisions and laid the foundations for the penetration of the State through the creation of mechanisms for political participation.

The meeting between Fidel Castro and Roberto Suarez marks the beginning of the symbiosis between international drug trafficking and the Havana regime.

Suarez's unusual and untimely withdrawal from criminal activity marked a devolution of criminal organizations, which returned to less sophisticated methods of indiscriminate violence and financial circulation. But without a doubt, the Castro-Suarez alliance marked an evolution for Cuba's doctrinal and operational practices, generating methods that served to finance, sustain and develop military operations in various conflicts such as those waged in Nicaragua, El Salvador, Panama, Colombia Peru, and Angola, among others.

The End of the Cold War?

It is clear that the end of the Cold War and the resultant lack of foreign exchange motivated the regimes that survived the fall of the Berlin Wall (Cuba and North Korea for example) to take more aggressive measures to obtain financial means.

The networks, the contacts and the know-how did not evaporate. In fact, one of the problems faced by the intelligence services of the West today lies in the erroneous idea that the Cold War implied the end of the operational capabilities developed by the Soviet Union and its allies.

Its trail can be clearly perceived when we review the individuals — both participants and facilitators — of the major international illicit networks today.

And Cuba?
Ochoa, De La Guardia and Trial Number 1 "Drug Trafficking, a Crime Without Borders"

Following these guidelines, the Cuban regime fully embraced illicit markets, assigning an essential role to the FAR (Revolutionary Armed Forces, in Spanish), at all levels, with clearly involved leaders such as the previously mentioned Admiral Santamaria, Chief of the Cuban Navy.

The investigation, documentation and revelation of these operations by President Ronald Reagan in May 1983 during a speech in Miami caused an unprecedented crisis in the highest circles of the Cuban government.

The rebuke by Granma didn't quash all the suspicions raised by Reagan's speech.[16] Moreover, the US government kept hammering away at the issue until 1988. When a new DEA operation uncovered an ongoing scheme, which involved some of the most prominent members of "la Corporación" and the highest level of the Cuban regime.

The reaction of the Cuban government to the evidence presented by the Reagan administration, which revealed the full participation of military institutions, government agencies and the Cuban intelligence apparatus in drug trafficking operations was rapid and brutal.

The most prominent military commander in Cuba's modern history, General Arnaldo Ochoa, was court-martialed and executed.

---

[16] Rafael Del Pino. *Los años de la guerra: Cinco mil días de sudor y sangre.* 2013

In addition, the head of the Convertible Currency Department, Antonio de la Guardia, was executed, and dozens of other officials of the State Security apparatus were sentenced to prison.

However, official explanations do not satisfy even the most basic process of contrast. The description provided by General Rafael Del Pino clearly reflects the situation:

> "There were 19 defendants, so it must have been necessary to confront each other's statements, confirm elements, verify aspects of what they were saying, repeat cross-examinations to confirm and specify information. And all that in just 3 or 4 days? Not even the KGB in close collaboration with the CIA and Scotland Yard achieve such speed and efficiency in such a complex case. The only thing that would have made possible the publication of this very fast and detailed report is that all the background information should be recorded in the archives of the Ministry of the Interior, because those were official operations of the Cuban government, perfectly controlled and directed by the high levels.

> Otherwise it is impossible to explain in thorough detail how the Cuban people and the world were informed on June 22nd by a *Granma* newspaper editorial."[17]

In fact, and despite all the containment measures applied by the government, even within the trial, evidence that linked Fidel Castro himself came to light.

> "The most embarrassing defense complicity occurred during the testimony of Captain Miguel Ruiz Po, when the defendant presented new evidence involving Fidel Castro in drug trafficking."[18]

---

[17] Rafael Del Pino. Op.cit.

[18] Ibid.

However, this event entailed neither the end of the operations nor the withdrawal of the Cuban regime from its participation in drug trafficking. On the contrary, the evolution, diversification and sophistication led them to venture into new ways of generating much needed income, such as trafficking in persons under near-slavery conditions, cyber-crime, money laundering and ultimately outsourcing drug trafficking operations through organizations such as the Revolutionary Armed Forces of Colombia (FARC) or co-opted governments such as the Chavista regime of Venezuela.

The Bolivian Model, One Can Always Learn

It is not uncommon in the history of conflicts that the boldest advances, eventually used in large-scale wars, first occur in places out of sight of the great powers--sometimes with eventual disastrous results for those powers (Vietnam and Afghanistan immediately come to mind).

Although an entire chapter of this paper will be devoted to the analysis of the model generated in Bolivia, it is worth briefly describing it.

In Bolivia, an insurgency born from an organization basically dedicated to an illicit venture (in this case the complete coca-cocaine circuit), turned that activity into the logistical base from which to finance a multi-pronged assault against a formal State:

The combination included an armed struggle to protect the deep rearguard (El Chapare, where coca is planted and cocaine is manufactured); a social protest movement to generate conflict in urban centers; cocaine trafficking and its benefits to generate corruption no longer as an end but as a method; and finally political quasi-legal action to seize power.

Once power was taken, the conflict was immediately continued as an end unto itself. There was no creation a social experiment, as has occurred with other revolutions. The purpose of the permanent conflict was to thwart the concentration of the enemy's means against the organization. The formal State became a tool at the service of the conflict, providing formal cover for money laundering of drug trafficking proceeds and political maneuvering both at the domestic and international levels.

A guiding principle commanding the operations of this phenomenon was permanent learning. All activities were subject to evaluation, a relentless and corporate type of evaluation, which was neither afraid to learn nor hesitant to apply what has been learned.

For this organization, conflict is permanent state of affairs, and the constant occurrence of conflict is key to the organization's survival.

The FARC and the Peace Process, Marquez and Santrich

The adoption of this model of war by the Revolutionary Armed Forces of Colombia might have been the subject of a heated debate within the organization's Secretariat. However, and perhaps ironically, the success of the Colombian State in neutralizing figures such as AKA Tirofijo, AKA Raul Reyes and AKA Mono Jojoy paved the way for its adoption.

There is no doubt that the evaluation carried out by the Secretariat and their allies in Havana showed that the classic conception of insurgency strategy and its implementation had been defeated militarily and politically by the democratic security strategy carried out by the government of Álvaro Uribe.

In order to avoid the collapse of the organization, it was decided to adopt the "Bolivian" model. The so-called peace process was established, a legal and partisan political action base was structured, and the organization of social movements and increased social protest conflict was launched.

25

At the same time, the emergence of a "dissent" was articulated with two characteristics: on the one hand, the retention of its armed capacity; and on the other, their presence at the centers of the coca-cocaine production circuit, which preserved its logistical and financial capacity. This dissent appeared in a curious way. It was a process — initially concealed but later made public — to connect with the National Liberation Army (ELN in Spanish), which de facto became the armed wing of the FARC, thus abandoning any pretense of ideological purity.

This strategic framework was supplemented by a consolidated base of operations outside the reach of the Colombian State. Coordinated by the Cuban forces, this platform is within Venezuelan territory and its true nature was clearly exposed when alias Iván Márquez and alias Jesús Santrich announced they were resuming the armed struggle exactly when their participation in the drug trafficking circuit was clearly demonstrated by United States and Colombian authorities.

Simultaneously, express statements were made by the Venezuelan regime in support of the rearmed FARC, an event unprecedented in the recent history of the hemisphere. They were openly endorsing the armed actions of a terrorist and drug trafficking organization in the territory of a neighboring State.[19]

The presentation by the Colombian authorities of a dossier with the evidence to demonstrate the points previously described, only reinforces the unique versatility of this model and its operational capabilities.[20]

---

[19] "Maduro apoya disisencia armada de FARC Colombia", *Diario de México*, Available at:
https://www.diariodemexico.com/maduro-apoya-disidencia-armada-de-farc-colombia

[20] "La denuncia que presentó el Gobierno contra Maduro en la OEA", El Tiempo, September 11, 2019. Available at:

Cubazuela

One of the prominent features of this war model is its quasi-modularity, which facilitates its export and reproduction requiring neither complex levels of logistical planning nor huge forces on the ground. The financial flow generated by the illicit ventures and a minimum of political traction are quite enough to proceed to its accelerated implementation. Corruption is a main method and institutional cooptation takes care of the rest, quickly destroying the institutional framework and generating conflict both internally and externally at the desired levels.

The most recent example of this feature is the dismal situation in Venezuela, as Blanco, Cartaya, Dominguez and Ocando described in relation to this South American nation in their seminal work "Cubazuela".

"What are we confronting in Venezuela? Venezuela is a failed State controlled by a criminal group linked to transnational drug trafficking and terrorism. That group has usurped institutions, dismantled democracy, snatched sovereignty from the people, and established a regime of terror. It continuously commits crimes against humanity, such as torture and genocide through the current famine and humanitarian disaster that plagues the population. Citizen insecurity added to political repression has left in 2018 more than 24,000 violent deaths — not including thousands who have died of malnutrition and lack of medicines — comparable to the sum of those in Afghanistan, Syria and Iraq for the same period. The exodus of three million people is analogous to that of Syria. It is a manmade regional catastrophe.

https://www.eltiempo.com/politica/gobierno/colombia-denuncia-en-la-oea-a-nicolas-maduro-411152

27

National independence has been surrendered to Cuba, which has established there a modern model of colonial domination. It has also ceded territories to foreign criminal groups (FARC, ELN, Hezbollah) in which laboratories for drug production have been installed. From Venezuela, the ELN directs its armed struggle against the Colombian State and plans terrorist actions such as the recent attack against the police academy in Bogotá.

The mass-produced drugs in these territories are then trafficked to countries, such as the United States and some members of the European Union, where people die each year from their use and where distribution bands contribute to raising crime rates. The narco State is also responsible for the mass exodus of more than three million people that today destabilizes the region economically and socially and creates the danger of a pandemic.

The situation in Venezuela, therefore, is unprecedented. We are not in the presence of an independent and sovereign State that controls its national territory, protects the welfare and security of its citizens and lives in peace with its neighbors. The State institutions have been transformed into perpetrators of a criminal enterprise."[21]

Hezbollah

The global reach of this new type of war becomes clear when an analysis of organizations like Hezbollah are followed, an organization that, according to the former director of the CIA, Mr. John Brennan, had become "very interesting":

---

[21] Juan Antonio Blanco, Rolando Cartaya, Luis Dominguez, Casto Ocando. *Cubazuela: Chronicle of a Cuban intervention.* Miami: Foundation for Human Rights in Cuba, 2019

"The Hezbollah External Security Organization (ESO), or unit 910 as it is known in the circles of the anti-terrorist community, is considered an elite unit among terrorist organizations. In recent years, ESO agents were apprehended while preparing to carry out attacks in Azerbaijan, Cyprus, Egypt, and Thailand, and in 2012 they successfully attacked a bus in Bulgaria on July 18th, precisely on the anniversary of the AMIA attack in Argentina. Bulgaria may seem far from Latin America, but the same network of Hezbollah terrorists planned attacks in Peru and Bolivia in 2014 and again in 2015.

Some of the ESO members who participated in these attempts are in fact connected to the AMIA attack in Argentina in 1994." [22]

But how does Hezbollah manage to operate on a global scale? How does Hezbollah evade the sanctions and containment and neutralization measures of highly capable States like Israel or the United States? The answer can be found in the following description of a large-scale operation carried out by the DEA called Cassandra:

"The campaign, called Operation Cassandra, was launched in 2008 after the United States anti-narcotics agency (DEA) accumulated sufficient evidence that Hezbollah had transformed from a Middle Eastern political-military organization to an international crime syndicate, whose financial capacity according to investigators reached one billion dollars annually from drug trafficking, arms smuggling, money laundering and other criminal activities.

For nearly eight years, DEA agents operating from a secret facility in Chantilly, Virginia, used interception, covert and

---

[22] Joseph M. Humire. *Argentina: Latin America's New Leader in Counterterrorism*, Gatestone Institute, July 2019

informative operations to map Hezbollah's criminal networks, all with the cooperation of 30 agencies of the
government of the United States as well as from friendly
countries.

These agents followed shipments of cocaine from Latin
America to West Africa and from there to Europe and the
Middle East, as well as other shipments through Venezuela
and Mexico to the United States. They also followed the
river of dirty money while it was being washed via the trade
of used cars to Africa among other cover-up activities.
With the cooperation of key witnesses, the agents discovered a vast conspiracy that led, according to the criteria of
the agents, directly to the highest level of Hezbollah as well
as their allies in Irán." [23]

The Bolivian Brazil, the cocaine airlift

As we have stated above, the Bolivian model generates a blueprint
of simple adaptation that can develop highly complex operations
while using all the resources of the underworld to give them the
necessary support.

This model can simultaneously generate cooperative networks in-
volving other related political actors who need these resources to
meet needs of a political nature, to pay bribes, or simply as a rein-
forcement of their "loyalty" and "revolutionary coherence".

Thus, in a world of laws it would normally be inconceivable that
Cuba could be able to literally occupy and control a State like Venezuela at will, or that Bolivia could essentially affect the Brazilian
colossus; however, the operation described below depicts in its
simplicity the level of sophistication reached:

---

[23] Josh Meyer. *The Secret Story of How Obama let Hezbollah off the Hook. Politico*, 2017

In his work *Hugo Chávez O Spectro*, journalist Leonardo Coutinho narrates in detail and with abundant proof how Bolivian air force planes as well as military personnel from Bolivia and Venezuela were used to transport cocaine from Bolivia to Venezuela and Cuba with final destination in the US. This case involved the co-ordination of Cuba and the circles of power of the Brazilian Workers' Party, the then ruling party the direct action of the Bolivarian Republic of Venezuela and the Plurinational State of Bolivia.

> "Morales and the Venezuelan president decided to rethink the operation and, instead of aircraft with Venezuelan registration, only aircraft of the Bolivian Air Force would cover the route, which would be called the ALBA route, in reference to the Bolivarian Alliance for the Peoples of Our America, the Chavista-inspired block, founded in 2004.

> At that meeting, in which the route was baptized, and its immediate start was determined, it was agreed that the costs would be fully covered by Caracas.

> Evo Morales appointed his Minister Juan Ramon Quintana as coordinator for the operation.

> To corroborate his version, Rocha detailed to DEA agents how Colonel Constanzo behaved as superior to all the Bolivian military assigned to the flights. He states that it was the Venezuelan who determined even the dates and routes of the flights.

> One of the most unusual orders issued by the Venezuelan was to avoid at all costs the Colombian airspace.

> For that, Rocha and the other pilots were forced to shift from one airway to another when they were in Brazil's airspace. Whenever they were in the Sao Gabriel da Cachoeira region, in the far north of Brazil, the pilots communicated the move to air traffic control. By moving to the

31

airway on the right, they avoided to fly over a country ruled by a president hostile to the interests of Caracas.

The pilot revealed that, on the return flights, the planes were fully loaded with anti-riot material, such as gas grenades, shields and rubber bullets. There were also sealed packages, which Rocha, a military with ample experience, knew that they were weapons and ammunition, whose final destination he claims not to know."

All the stealth that surrounded the operation led Rocha to suspect that it was being used to cover up crimes. At the end of 2010 he got the gap needed to find out what was being transported in the boxes designated as diplomatic pouch. In La Paz, Rocha had been ordered to transport a cargo of books, which was being sent to Havana by the Cuban ambassador, Rafael Dausá Céspedes.

The weight and volume of the material suggested that Dausá was transferring an entire library to his home country.

When the first stopover was made at the Libertador Air Base, more than 100 km from Caracas, Rocha saw that Venezuelans were unloading the cargo designated as diplomatic pouch that he had to transport to Cuba.

I claimed that there was an error, that those boxes could not be unloaded.

But the Venezuelan officers not only ignored me, they also proceeded to rebuke me with a ferocity that even my superiors would not dare to use against me."

Without an alibi, the Bolivian officer chose to remain silent.

As a result of his humiliation and shame, Rocha resolved to disobey the instructions received from his superiors and his own conservation instinct.

After delivering the flight plan to the control tower at the military base, he saw that the boxes unloaded from his plane were abandoned in the hangar.

Without any vigilance present at that time and believing that he would not be discovered, he broke the wrapping of one of the compartments and saw his cargo for the first time.

Instead of books there were packages of cocaine.

The Bolivian military claims that he was gasping for breath as a result. With strong chest pressure, he returned to the command booth to regain his composure before taking off for Cuba." [24]

The Bolivian Air Force officer who provided this testimony is co-operating with the federal agencies; and the data revealed has yet to be shared by the United States authorities. It is expected that the potential damage it could cause will result in new and more complex levels of response to the criminal organizations involved in the plot.

A Plane in the Desert of Mali

This way of war is not only limited to the Western Hemisphere, rather the scope is global and their ability to generate conflict is on a scale never seen before, challenging the capabilities of formal states.

When US Secretary of State Hillary Clinton described the situation in Mali in October 2012 as "critical" and asked regional leaders to deploy troops to counteract the growing presence of Al Qaeda in

---

[24] Leonardo Coutinho. *Hugo Chavez, O Espectro: Como o Presidente Venezuelano Alimentou o Narcotráfico Financiou o Terrorismo e Promoveu a Desordem Global*, 2018

the Maghreb (AQIM), she was actually confirming a new theater of operations for this mode of conflict:

> "There is concrete evidence of the linkage of Al Qaeda and the trafficking of cocaine in the Sahara," said Dr. Kwesi Aning, director of academic affairs and research at the Koffi Annan Peace Operations Training Center in Ghana. "In the beginning, drug trafficking was dominated by Touaregs and intermediaries who guided traffickers to fuel depots and water reservoirs in the desert. But after Al Qaeda began to engage in drug trafficking approximately ten years ago, we have seen a massive increase in the amount of cocaine involved. They have both the networks and the logistic know-how.

> The lack of legal control was blamed in the incident called 'air cocaine', when a Boeing 727 believed to be transporting about ten tons of cocaine was found half scorched in the middle of the Mali desert.

> The British Organized Crime Agency investigation group reported that a plane from Venezuela had landed in Mali and that its cargo had been transported by 4x4 vehicles to Timbuktu before the authorities lost its trail."[25]

What You Thought You Knew, and the true reach of Odebrecht

The analysis of the Odebrecht scandal has been limited to one-dimension, focusing exclusively on classic corruption.

However, data published by journalists such as Leonardo Coutinho or Sasha Chavkin show that the Odebrecht affair has much deeper

---

[25] Afua Hirsch, "Cocaine Flows through Sahara as Al-Qaida Cashes in on Lawlessness", *The Guardian,* May 2, 2013

implications. The scope of the scandal is clearly much more than a mere corruption scandal.

What is hidden under the Odebrecht corruption facade is probably the largest ever, most complex operation of money and asset laundering, as well as capital triangulation via large-scale construction contracts often generated by governments that ended up benefiting groups of the transnational organized crime, terrorism and other actors hostile to the United States.

The Mariel Port

Perhaps one of the clearest cases is that of the port of Mariel terminal in Cuba, whose construction, operation and related incidents provide insight into these complex operations and their nature in the context of a conflict.

At the beginning, the project was estimated to cost 220 million US dollars; later on, the Dubai Ports World company entered into negotiations with the Cuban government and the cost of building the port terminal began to increase exponentially.

The testimony of the manager in charge of this project reflects the genesis of the Mariel saga:

> "Finally, a deal was negotiated with the Cuban counterpart, led by the anointed one, in which a joint venture for 25 years would be signed. It was a 51:49 shareholding ratio in which Cuba would only have to invest 20 percent of the capital required for the project, whose total amounted to US $ 350 million for the construction of the entire port: dredging, construction, equipment and operating capital."[26]

---

[26] Stephen Purvis, *Close But No Cigar. A True Story of Prison Life in Castro's Cuba*, London: Weidenfeld & Nicolson, 2018

However, following an order from Cuba's highest political level, the contract was unilaterally terminated, but:

> "Only three months later my former Cuban partners had already signed an agreement with a Brazilian company financed by a loan provided by the Brazilian State, and the amount of the credit for the construction of the same project was 850 million US dollars. Now, that raises an obvious question. What was the extra half billion for?"[27]

This project had been a personal request of by Hugo Chavez to Lula Da Silva. The irregularities in it, not only tainted the political prestige of the former Brazilian president but also implicated one of the strongest institutions in Brazil, the Development Bank of Brazil — BNDES — equivalent to the Exim Bank in the United States.

The amounts disbursed by the Brazilian treasury totaled 1.2 billion dollars, and although the BNDES was fully aware, did not stand up to scrutiny, even if you added up all the bilateral trade between Cuba and Brazil. It certainly did not comply with Brazilian law or BNDES statutes.[28]

Another part of this global operation was located in the streets of Sao Paulo and in the shops controlled by Hezbollah at the Triple Border. According to information collected during the Brazilian authorities' investigation, the capital flow through Odebrecht exceeded the capacity of any formal financial institution and caused them to acquire their own bank. At the same time, the capital demands in different currency denominations developed into a strategic alliance between the informal currency exchange houses

---

[27] Ibid.

[28] Leonardo Coutinho, "Conta dos empréstimos do BNDES para o Porto de Mariel não fecha", *Veja,* August 30, 2015. Available at: https://veja.abril.com.br/politica/a-conta-dos-emprestimos-do-bndes-para-o-porto-de-mariel-nao-fecha/

in Brazil (better known as Doleiros) controlled by Hezbollah, co-caine traffickers of the Bolivian government, the local PCC (*Primeiro Comando da Capital*, in Portuguese) and the highest ranks of Odebrecht's Divisao de Operacoes Estruturadas, that is to say, the heart of the operation.

Enter the Dragon:
The role of China in the new model

The Chinese strategic doctrine has two sides; one of them is formal and embodies its intention to generate a "comprehensive national power" that seeks the following strategic objectives:

- Perpetuate the model under the direction of the PCC.
- Maintain internal stability.
- Generate economic growth and development.
- Defend national sovereignty and territorial integrity.
- Ensure the status of China as a power with global reach. [29]

The other side is explained in a seminal work that Chinese military commanders have carried out with increasing success and is reflected in their work entitled *Unrestricted War*, authored by Qiao Liang and Wang Xiansui. It not only recognizes China's lack of capability to match the United States in the conventional military realm, but also provides a very clear analysis of non-State actors and their ability to generate situations of "non-military war" against potential enemies, the characteristics of which makes their tactics attractive models to imitate. Their discussion and analysis of Pablo Escobar and the Colombian cartels is very interesting in this regard.

Qiao and Wang go even further and argue that "the battlefield has fundamentally changed. It is no longer a space in which military

---

[29] Defense Intelligence Agency. *China Military Power, Modernizing a Force to Fight and Win*, 2019.

forces confront each other. Instead, society itself has become the battlefield. They argue that the wars of the future will inevitably encompass all elements of society without limits.[30]

For China, this new model is an advance in its capabilities. This, combined with its enormous financial mobilization capability, the lack of any type of checks and balances or external controls, enables China not only to participate in, but also to encourage questionable practices, by facilitating payments, providing credits, creating companies and establishing presence through multiple actors. This includes "entrepreneurs" with high level education, and technical skill, a high level of cultural understanding of the places where they are sent and solid military and/or intelligence backgrounds.

These operatives have been deployed globally, and can be detected without much effort in such dissimilar places as Angola, Yemen, Bolivia or Argentina.

A recent interesting development are reports that China used elements of criminal organizations to contain and neutralize the opposition in the Hong Kong protests.

How Much Money is it?

There is no clear understanding of how much money is generated through the use of the underworld as an essential factor in this new type of war, the overall impact that this activity on security, in the United States, the Western Hemisphere, and much less the security implications on a global scale.

---

[30] Qiao Liang and Wang Xiangsui. *Unrestricted Warfare*. Beijing: PLA Literature and Arts Publishing House, 1999)

However, the example below revealing the return of a single operation during a single year of activity will give us a good indication of what we face.

According to CNN reporters Nick Paton, Natallie Gallon and Diana Castrillon "drug trafficking from Venezuela to the United States is in full swing, even in the middle of that country's political and economic debacle. Simultaneously, officials of the United States government as well as other governments in the region have indicated that the military and political elite of the Venezuelan regime facilitate drug trafficking through the country aboard hundreds of light aircraft."

According to the same report citing official sources, the volume of cocaine from Colombia, traversing Venezuela to the United States reached 240 metric tons in 2018, representing profits of nearly 39 billion US dollars in a single year.

Some officials consulted by CNN indicated that this estimate is very conservative in terms of the amount of narcotics transported via this route.

End Game

This analysis leads us to some conclusions. These are by no means simple and still subject to debate and refinement. They are not pleasant and will probably bother many readers. **The first conclusion is that the new model cannot be replicated by us, its adversaries, without losing the very essence of who we are.**

Our biggest limitation to combating it is that we, the West, have not yet understood the nature of this new model and more seriously, for ideological/philosophical reasons several countries refuse to accept its existence.

These circumstances cause countries such as the United States to limit the scope of its response, often restricting it to the law enforcement and judicial arena, which provides our adversaries ample room for reaction, adaptation and maneuver.

It is vital to our future to neutralize this new model for an even more profound reason:

> **The West will never be able to adopt this model of war, due to the foundation of Western society on institutional norms and the checks and balances inherent in a democracy.**

This model, that violates every principle of law, participates fully in the illicit underworld and violates the most fundamental human rights without fear of consequences, has no way of being adapted, imitated or employed by the democracies of the world.

However, it can be defeated as long as it is understood that we face a different, innovative and bold model of war, but one that even in all its potential has less resources than countries such as the United States.

It is necessary to rethink our operational and doctrinal models so that the institutional response of the West can best employ its military and non-military capabilities to counter this total and endless war in a holistic manner. Otherwise we will be faced with the dilemma that the model developed by the freest and most capable societies and institutions in terms of generating progress in history will for the first time be overcome, surpassed and defeated.

Terror and Crime
Lenin, Qutb and Illicit Economies

David E. Spencer, PhD

Dr. David Spencer is an associate professor at the William J. Perry Center. From 2014-2017 he was on detail as the Colombia/South America desk officer at the Office of the Secretary of Defense Counternarcotics & Global Threats. He also served from 2011-2012 as the Colombia Policy Director in the Office of the Secretary of Defense Western Hemisphere Affairs. Dr. Spencer earned his doctorate in Political Science from George Washington University in 2002 where he studied Latin American Politics, specializing in regional insurgency and terrorism. He earned his MA and BA (both in International Relations) from Brigham Young University in 1992 and 1988 respectively.

Before accepting his current position at the Perry Center, Dr. Spencer was Director of Combating Terrorism at Hicks & Associates. In this position he supported several USOUTHCOM projects. For the last 15 years he has worked in a variety of positions in Support of Plan Colombia. He spent five years in El Salvador as a consultant to the Ministry of Defense during the recent civil war.

Dr. Spencer has worked for a number of think-tanks and consulting firms, such as Center for Naval Analyses (CNA) and Science Applications International Corporation (SAIC). Dr. Spencer was raised in Latin America, living in Chile, Costa Rica, Colombia, Venezuela, and Guatemala. Dr. Spencer served in the US Army and National Guard as an Infantryman. He attained the rank of Sergeant and was mobilized for the First Gulf War in 1990-1991. In June 2011, he published the study Colombia's Road to Recovery: Security and Governance 1982-2010. He was awarded the Exceptional Public Service Medal in 2013. He is a military history and archaeology buff.

The United States doesn't like it when our enemies don't fight by our rules. While this should not surprise anyone, what is surprising is how difficult it often is to convince US government officials to accept that our rivals have developed strategies and methods that completely bypass the treaties, conventions, institutions, and capabilities we have invested so much effort into creating and building up. It seems that we have difficulty accepting that our rivals are as intelligent, and sometimes even more intelligent than we are, and that they could develop methods of conflict that are successful and much more cost effective than our own. Convincing them is precisely the objective of the present volume.

From 2002 to 2005, I worked as part of what was known as the Defense Adaptive Red Team or DART. The purpose of DART was to try to get inside the mind of the United States' rivals and attempt to simulate them in a series of exercises and studies done to help the regional combatant commands prepare and plan for current and future scenarios. To prepare for these exercises I spent hundreds of hours investigating the philosophies, thinking, values and actions of various rivals around the world. Although unable to completely adopt their way of thinking — because I could not get outside of my own culture, education and experience — I feel I was able to make a significant approximation. What impressed me from my deep dives on our challengers and participation in the exercises "against" our own forces was the following:

First, the tendency of the US and by extension, Western powers, to underestimate the intelligence and capabilities of our enemies. Just because our enemies often don't have formal education or don't wear western-style clothes, does not mean that they're not intelligent or dangerous. Some of the most sophisticated insurgent philosophy, thinking and strategy that I ever read came from laptops captured deep in the jungles of Colombia, written by people that wear rubber boots for shoes, while sitting at improvised desks made of bamboo. One of the most sophisticated and well thought out insurgent strategies — described elsewhere in this volume — that I have ever studied was developed by the Cocaleros of Bolivia.

This is not to say that every member of these groups is equally intelligent or sophisticated. A hostage kidnapped by the Colombian FARC described to me with derision how his captors thought the special effects stunts in the movie *The Matrix* were real and asked him how people learned to do that. This type of interaction is probably why Western powers underestimate their rivals. However, care should be taken to avoid thinking that the foot soldiers of an organization — with whom there is often the most interaction — are representative of the leadership. The leadership are often highly educated, both formally and self-taught, and differently motivated than the bulk of their members. This is not that much of a leap of logic, and is quite normal in our own large organizations and institutions. For example, the motives and thinking of Army privates is often very different from that of their generals.

However, for some reason this is often overlooked when dealing with insurgents. Perhaps, this is because of propaganda perpetuated by the insurgents themselves such as Che Guevara's musings about the "New Man"[31], and while his assertions may be partially true, especially early in a group's history, when there are fewer than a dozen highly dedicated members — the "mythological" stage of most insurgencies about which there is often abundant literature — it is not so true in later stages when there are hundreds, if not thousands of insurgents, which are often not as well documented.

---

[31] Che Guevara, *Socialism and Man in Cuba*, 1965. Available at: https://www.marxists.org/archive/guevara/1965/03/man-socialism.htm, accessed on September 25, 2019

Second, the problem of "Mirror Imaging." This is probably the most common error when analyzing enemy groups. It is the tendency to project onto the enemy the same organization, motivations and training that we have, and/or more importantly the same values and logic. Our favorite enemies have been the Nazis and the Soviets, because they looked a lot like us. They were relatively easy to understand, so we want to make other enemies look like us too.

For example, the initial analyses of Al Qaeda showed line and block charts that looked very similar to charts used to represent the organization and structure of conventional Western military units. While, not totally incorrect, the implication of those line and block charts were that Al Qaeda operated similar to conventional military units. That was simply not true except very vaguely. The analysts had "mirror-imaged." Subsequently, as more was learned about Al Qaeda, analysts developed the spider web-like network graphics that people are familiar with today. This has been a much more useful tool to understand and combat Al Qaeda.

Mirror imaging is not only limited to organization and structure. Often, enemy's values are also confused with our own. For example, the United States places a premium on human life and will go to extraordinary measures to protect life to the point of sacrificing large amounts of equipment and even other lives to save a single individual. On the other hand, our enemies often don't place as high a value on human life and will trade one or many human lives to achieve some end that would not be worth it to us. For example, often, our enemies will sacrifice several lives to save particular items of equipment, because the equipment is scarce and thus valued above human lives.

Another example is a conversation I had in 1999 with a prominent and influential Colombian analyst in which he insisted that FARC's strategic objective could not possibly be to take power because the Cold War had ended, Communism had proved unviable, and the Soviet Union had disappeared. He maintained this position despite the fact that recently captured FARC documents spoke of taking power and imposing a Communist government. He and many others dismissed the documents because they didn't think that what they advocated were realistic objectives in the post-Cold War world. Whether the stated FARC objective was realistic or not was immaterial. What was material was that this objective was what was causing the FARC to subject Colombia to a campaign of extreme violence. Because of this, they had to be taken at their written and verbal word. It was not until the Colombian government took the FARC objectives seriously that they were able to develop the appropriate strategy to defeat them. Experience with the FARC and other groups has taught me that what an enemy group writes, particularly in the documents intended for their internal consumption, actually does represent their objectives, values and intentions, regardless of their actual ability to achieve those things.

Third, there is a significant body of literature that our enemy's read to learn how to combat the United States and the West. Some of this literature is produced internally, but much of it, particularly the reference documents, have been produced externally. The various organizations communicate, share and learn from each other, often without regard to ideology. This is particularly true of Marxist and Islamic groups.

Between 2001 and 2003 some terrorism analysts claimed that Islamic terrorism, as represented by Al Qaeda, was so different from anything that came before that it was useless to reference previous Marxist and secular insurgent and terrorist groups to be able to understand them. Another one of these analysts tried to interpret everything they did through the Quran, and likewise claimed that it was unproductive to study previous groups to gain insight into Al Qaeda and Islamic groups.

However, as I studied Al Qaeda, there seemed to be a lot of things in common with previous groups. A lot of the thinking and explanations reminded me a great deal of the Bolsheviks, the

Vietnamese and even the Cuban-inspired Latin American *focos*. The aforementioned analysts were largely those that had sprung up right around September 11, 2001 and as far as I could tell, had only done in-depth studies of Islamic groups. They had impressive knowledge about these groups. However, they had only done cursory reviews of previous groups and had essentially dismissed them. I was new to the study of extremist Islamic groups, but had a lot of knowledge about Marxist and secular Arab groups during the Cold War. As a result, I made connections that they didn't. However, because I was not an expert on Islamic terrorism, and unsure of what I was seeing, I held my judgment, but nevertheless noted the coincidences. I thought that maybe in thinking about similar problem sets, the Islamic groups had independently come to the same conclusions as the Marxists.

It was not long after that Al Qaeda and other group's documents were captured in Iraq, Afghanistan and elsewhere. I was not surprised when it was discovered that they contained extensive and very recognizable excerpts from Mao and Che Guevara. Even Sayyid Qutb's writings showed extensive influence from the Bolshevik's such as the idea of a revolutionary vanguard and so forth. While these excerpts were not attributed to their original authors, the sources were unmistakable.

Certainly, their ideology was Islamic and not Marxist, but much of their methodology was taken from the Marxist playbook. This syncretism between radical Islamic ideas and Marxism is in fact, what made them so dangerous. Daesh or ISIS shows a similar combination of Islamic ideas and Marxist methods. In fact, the manual *How to Survive in the West: A Mujahid Guide* (2015) — available at the time of this writing on several different websites — demonstrates a very sophisticated and thorough understanding of Marxist revolutionary methodology walking the would-be Jihadist through the Marxist developed process from being a lone wolf, through the formation of a terrorist cell, the development and interaction with social protest movements, how to organizing a guerrilla group, the advance from guerrilla to mobile to positional warfare and then the triumph of the revolution. To add to its sophistication, they have pushed these ideas into the 21st Century, walking the reader through the technical aspects of the use of the dark web and so forth.[32] This manual is so well done that I use it as a reference document to teach my students about Marxist thinking on revolution. What I used to teach employing about ten different readings is available in a single document written by Islamic Jihadists.

This syncretism between Marxist revolutionary methodology and radical Islam may surprise many because of the apparent incompatibility of the ideologies, one being anti-religious atheist, and the other hyper theocratic — after all the development of the latter got a significant boost during the war against the Soviet occupation of Afghanistan, when the two ideologies went to war against each other. It is logical to think that both sides would have developed anti-bodies that would cause the adherents to reject each other out of hand like Democracy does with National Socialism. Yet, in some parts of the world today, not only is there a syncretism between their doctrines, but alliances of purpose as well.

In Latin America, the Socialist governments of Cuba, Venezuela, Bolivia and the Kirchner government of Argentina, have maintained close relationships with Iran, both allowing Iranian operatives to work in their countries as well as sending cadre to Iran to go through training in Special Operations and Security. Similarly, Hezbollah has enjoyed free reign throughout the region, largely shielded by the same socialist governments and even non-socialist but leftist leaning governments.[33] While this relationship

---

[32] *ISIS, How to Survive in the West: A Mujahid Guide* (2015). Available at: https://archive.org/download/inside_213/INSIDE.pdf, accessed on September 25, 2019.

[33] See Joseph Humire, *Iran and Hezbollah In the Western Hemisphere: Written Testimony before US House of Representatives Committee on Foreign Affairs Subcommittee on The Western Hemisphere (WHEM) Subcommittee on The Middle East & North Africa (MENA)*, March 18, 2015.

between Marxism and Shiite radicals is well documented, there are also strong rumors about the presence of Sunni radicals such as Daesh or Al-Shabaab, but they are not yet sufficiently documented.

This combination or coincidence has not been limited to Latin America as in Syria, the Iranians and Russians have both been providing assistance in the form of money, equipment, military/paramilitary personnel, diplomatic and moral support to the Assad regime. This may respond to a somewhat different logic, but is nonetheless a case where we see the two very opposed ideologies working in coordination for a common interest.

These strange syncretisms and combinations go back to the point that is trying to be made. While perhaps incompatible ideologically, these different political philosophies share a common enemy, the Westphalian system of states dominated by the United States. Should they defeat their main foe, they well might turn on each other, but for now they collaborate in important ways because they recognize that a combination of efforts is more likely to achieve their strategic goals than to fight separately. As the old saying goes, "the enemy of my enemy is my friend." Furthermore, it is the combinations and syncretisms that make these organizations truly dangerous and give them operational flexibility they otherwise wouldn't enjoy.

In the late 1990s, I had returned from Colombia to the United States and was asked to stop by US Southern Command to brief the staff on what I had observed. During the presentation a great debate broke out between the staff over whether the FARC were an insurgent organization or a drug trafficking organization. This debate became quite heated because if they were a drug trafficking organization, then a particular set of laws and resources could be used against them, and if they were an insurgency, then it required the application of a different set of resources. I finally intervened in the heated discussion and pointed out to the staff that what made the FARC truly dangerous was that they were both an insurgency and a drug trafficking organization. This gave them both resources and maneuver room that they would not have otherwise enjoyed if they had been purely one or the other. It was not their problem that they were a combination of both. It was the United States' problem because we had divided the two aspects into mutually exclusive boxes. We were the ones having the dilemma, not them, which allowed them to operate in the institutional gaps or seams of our system. It was not until 2003 that Congress passed the 1021 authority that recognized the intimate connection between narcotics and the insurgent organizations and authorized money for Plan Colombia (counternarcotics money) to be used to combat Colombian organizations on the list of terrorist organizations (FARC, ELN and AUC).

The relationship between narcotics and Marxist insurgency was nothing new. Mao obtained money for the Chinese revolution through the Opium and Heroin trade. However, it didn't develop into a major source of resources because the Soviets began financing Mao starting in the 1930s. The relationship between the Marxist Cuban government and narcotics began early in the Cold War. There is documented evidence going back at least as early as 1966. In that year, the Tricontinental Conference endorsed narcotics trafficking as a means to undermine Western society.[34] These ideas became deeds at least as early as 1984, if not before, when it was discovered that the Cubans had developed a drug running network that involved the Colombian Medellin Cartel, the Colombian M-19 guerrillas, Panama's dictator Manuel Noriega, the Nicaraguan Sandinista government and the Cuban regime.[35]

Narcotics trafficking was not only a good way to undermine Western societies, but to make a lot of money to finance Marxist revolutions. Nevertheless, the US Ambassador to Colombia, Lewis

---

[34] Rachel Ehrenfeld, *Narco-Terrorism and the Cuban Connection*, Washington, DC: The Cuban American National Foundation, 1988, p. 10.

[35] Ibid, pp. 1-9.

Tambs, was mocked at the time for coining the term "narco-terrorists" to describe the Colombian M-19 and its relationship to the Medellin Cartel. Although nobody denied the evidence, these connections were seen as occasional and episodic versus as an integral and systematic way to finance revolution. This was because Socialism was considered a moral philosophy and therefore incompatible, except temporarily, with organized crime.

Even as late as 1999, despite significant physical and documentary evidence, US government officials were extremely reluctant to recognize how much the FARC was financed by narcotics trafficking because the FARC was a political insurgency and surely, it was reasoned, were it known that they were heavily involved in drug trafficking, it would seriously impact their ability to gain the support of the Colombian people. While, it did impact their ability to attract popular support, it did not stop the FARC from continuing or evening deepening their involvement in drug trafficking. The resources from drug trafficking allowed the FARC to develop the creation of a nearly conventional guerrilla army that could go toe to toe with the Colombian military and often win, despite the fact that their popular support was always lacking. Their military prowess was always far out of proportion to their political acumen. It was only between 2001-2003, that FARC's general relationship and dependence on drug trafficking became broadly accepted by virtually all Colombia analysts.

Fortunately for the Colombian government and the United States, despite these massive resources, FARC played right into US and western hands. They used the money to develop a large-scale military organization, just the kind of organization that US counterinsurgency doctrine had been designed to combat. Once the nature of the threat was recognized and a serious political commitment to combat it using mainstream counterinsurgency methodology was made, it was just a matter of time before FARC was defeated... unless they adapted. Between 2003 and 2014, they

refused to adapt, and predictably, since US and Colombian government political will and resources were sustained, the FARC
were systematically defeated.

In 1906, Vladimir Lenin wrote:

> "Let us begin from the beginning. What are the fundamen-
> tal demands which every Marxist should make of an
> examination of the question of forms of struggle? In the
> first place, Marxism differs from all primitive forms of so-
> cialism by not binding the movement to any one particular
> form of struggle. It recognizes the most varied forms of
> struggle; and it does not "concoct" them, but only general-
> izes, organizes, gives conscious expression to those forms
> of struggle of the revolutionary classes which arise of
> themselves in the course of the movement. Absolutely hos-
> tile to all abstract formulas and to all doctrinaire recipes,
> Marxism demands an attentive attitude to the mass struggle
> in progress, which, as the movement develops, as the class-
> consciousness of the masses grows, as economic and polit-
> ical crises become acute, continually gives rise to new and
> more varied methods of defense and attack. Marxism,
> therefore, positively does not reject any form of strug-
> gle."[36]

In summary, what Lenin says is that there is no fixed formula for
making revolution, and therefore revolutionaries cannot be rigid
about the methods they use if they want to succeed. They need to
be flexible in the application of various methods and do whatever
helps the revolution win. Given that this paragraph was written
over 113 years ago, I am always a bit perplexed when people in
the west are so surprised that our enemies — many of them educated and inspired either fully or in part by Marxist revolution-

---

[36] Vladimir I Lenin, *Guerrilla Warfare*, 1906. Available at https://www.marx-
ists.org/archive/lenin/works/1906/gw/i.htm#v11pp65-213 accessed on
September 23, 2019.

aries — deviate from the "rule book" and come up with new ways of "struggle."

I think two things are at fault. First, very few read the foundational Marxist documents. Many thinks that they are anachronistic and don't apply to the situation today. It is my belief that quite to the contrary, they apply at least as much today as they did ten to thirty years ago. Yes, circumstances have changed, but the general principles are still being applied today and even being revamped.

Second, Western powers have invested huge fortunes in developing military and security apparatus to combat our enemies in ways that we are comfortable fighting them (the aforementioned example of FARC). We want our enemies to remain static and play by our rules. What we don't want to recognize is that one of the prices of victory is that your rivals will seek new and different ways to defeat you in the future. This means that if we intend to remain victorious, we must never rest on our laurels and become complacent.

Since the Cold War ended in 1989-1990, the United States has been the single world hegemon. We have militarily defeated challenger after challenger in Kuwait, Bosnia, Kosovo, Afghanistan, Iraq multiple times, Libya, and others. We have helped our allies defeat their challengers in El Salvador, Colombia, the Philippines and elsewhere. Despite all of these victories, the enemies of the United States are smart and adaptive. It is folly to underestimate them. They are seeking ways to defeat the vast economic and military power of this country. They are actively working to overthrow the international system essentially created and maintained by the United States. Since they cannot compete with the might of the United States conventionally, and even in irregular combat, they are seeking other ways to neutralize and overcome the awesome power that we possess. They are finding ways to do battle with that minimizes their weaknesses and maximizes their strengths, in other words other ways besides traditional warfare to combat United States power. Evidence that they are experiencing success in their quest is the fact that our military victories are increasingly fleeting, unclear, indefinite, and our conflicts are becoming increasingly prolonged. Furthermore, even though we are often enjoying very clear military victories at the tactical level, it is becoming increasingly difficult to achieve the corresponding political victory to make that military win have a strategic outcome. In the end, our military victories on the battlefield are irrelevant if we cannot achieve corresponding political victories as the Vietnamese so painfully taught us.[37]

Again, we must turn to the Marxists to understand what is going on. A misunderstood concept — sometimes by even some Marxists — is what is known as the "combination of all forms of struggle." This Maoist idea, later perfected by the Vietnamese, was that revolutionary domination was achieved through the simultaneous application of various tools. This involved both violent and non-violent means. Whether violence or non-violence predominated and within either area, which specific method of violence or non-violence predominated, depended entirely on which method, under local circumstances, would advance the organization closest to political domination.[38]

We need to emphasize that violence under the combination of all forms of struggle has a very particular role. Violence is a means of establishing space so that non-violent means can be employed to establish political domination. The main justification for the use of violence is that the regimes have shut off political space off to the would-be revolutionaries, so they have no other choice but to resort to violence as a principle method of action to pry open that

---

[37] By David T. Zabecki, "Colonel Harry G. Summers, Jr., was a soldier, scholar, military analyst, writer, editor and friend." Available at: http://www.clausewitz.com/readings/SummersObitText.htm, accessed on September 10, 2019.

[38] Thomas A. Marks & Paul B. Rich (2017) "Back to the future – people's war in the 21st century," *Small Wars & Insurgencies,* 28:3, 409-425, DOI: 10.1080/09592318.2017.1307620

space. This is evident in many insurgent's manifestos, such as that of the FARC.

> "We are revolutionaries who fight for a change of regime. We wanted to and struggled for that change using the least painful way for our people, the peaceful way, the democratic struggle of the masses, the legal way that is outlined in the Colombian Constitution. That path was violently closed, and as we are revolutionaries that in one way or another play the historical role that we were destined for, obligated by the circumstances described above, we were forced to find another way: the road of armed revolution to struggle for power."[39]

The FARC and many other insurgencies that were eventually defeated, made the mistake of overemphasizing the armed struggle at the expense of other forms of struggle, and forgetting its particular role to open up space for the non-violent or political elements. The armed struggle itself became an end unto itself, rather than a tool for political struggle. So, despite solving their resource problem via drug trafficking, the FARC were never able to develop the kind of political struggle that they wished for or needed to remain viable. This is why they were forced to negotiate a peace agreement that was signed at the end of 2016.

The FARC were not the only ones. Many groups made armed struggle the default solution for political change, rather than a tool of last resort, or even one tool among many, and as a consequence many armed groups lost the political support and legitimacy they were seeking. In part, this was driven by the dynamics of the Cold War, internal political change caught between the competition for domination between two world powers. This made compromise difficult and exacerbated the violence of these internal struggles.

---

[39] FARC, *Programa Agrario de los Guerrilleros,* July 20, 1964. Available at: http://www.cedema.org/ver.php?id=4021 accessed September 25, 2019.

In the post-Cold War world, many of those dynamics changed. Internal conflicts were no longer overshadowed by a global rivalry. In Latin America this led to the establishment of democracies in every country except Cuba. However, because they were incipient, many of them were very weak. Despite democratization, this made them vulnerable to being overthrown. On the other hand, the fall of the Soviet Union meant that there was no longer financing and resources available for insurgent organizations from outside, so even though the new democracies were weak, there was little stomach to sponsor insurgency in the international arena. Yet insurgency did not disappear in Latin America. There was the previously mentioned FARC in Colombia along with their compatriots, the ELN. In Peru, Sendero Luminoso was strong, there was insurgency in Guatemala that was still languishing without external support, and finally there was an incipient group in Paraguay that would eventually become People's Paraguayan Army or the EPP.

With the exception of the Guatemalans that were in the process of seeking a final peace agreement, all of them took advantage of criminal economies, particularly drug trafficking to fund their armed structures and prosecute traditional insurgency focused on the armed struggle. While this allowed them to continue their armed activities, and in some cases reach new levels of violence to challenge to the state, the error they all made was to fail to recognize that the political door was no longer slammed shut.

These insurgencies failed to understand that since political circumstances had changed, maybe a different mix of the combination of all forms of struggle was called for. In their analyses, the democratization of the region changed nothing, therefore the continuation of primarily armed insurgency was imperative. Overall, by the time of this writing, this mode of insurgency has been defeated, because the United States and its allies know how to confront it.

It was the Bolivian cocaleros who figured out the new context, applied the principles of insurgency to their reality and developed a new combination of struggle that took advantage of the new dynamics, without exposing themselves to the strengths of the Western powers. Angered by US sponsored coca eradication they decided to take power. Because there was political space available, instead of armed violence as the main method of struggle, violent social protest was adopted. This was brilliant because the state could not prevent it, and had few tools to combat it without losing legitimacy both internally and externally. Furthermore, it neutralized the state's main counterrevolutionary tool, the Bolivian military. They couldn't send infantry battalions to fight against a social protest without suffering fatal political delegitimization. However, the violence and scale of the protests made it difficult to act with traditional police forces alone.

The reason this method had not been very successful before, is because traditional social protest faced a significant problem; which is that it could not usually be sustained over time because eventually people had to eat. In order to eat, they had to go back to work, which meant ending the protest. Thus, the second plank of the Bolivian combination of forms of struggle was to fund social protest with drug trafficking proceeds. Having solved the problem of financing, and thus able to sustain social mobilization nearly indefinitely, the protests had a much more powerful impact, because the government could not depend on them eventually running out of steam. This meant that unless the government could break the protest up quickly, they almost invariably had to negotiate with, and make concessions to the protesters.

The armed component did not cease, but rather took on a very specific supporting role, and that was to protect the drug industry, the main source of funding, from US sponsored counternarcotics operations. This filled the coffers of the cocaleros which then allowed them to fund social protests and other political activities. For example, the cocaleros were able to fund the creation of a political party which then consolidated the gains of the violent social protests through electoral politics and the promulgation of laws.

Over a period of ten years, this combination of the forms of struggle led to the siege of the capital La Paz by masses of social protesters, the resignation of President Gonzalo Sanchez de Lozada and the convocation of early elections that led to the election of the cocalero candidate, Evo Morales. This case of insurgency is described in greater depth in another part of this volume.

The important point is the brilliant way that the Bolivian cocaleros applied the tried and tested principles of Marxist insurgency to a new context, came up with an innovative combination of forms of struggle that led to a revolutionary triumph. The same kind of brilliant thinking has been applied to subsequently consolidating an authoritarian state while maintaining a façade of democracy that has perpetuated the cocaleros in power for over 14 years in Bolivia as of this writing. Similar thinking brought to power and has sustained a similar regime for 20 years in Venezuela.

The current severe economic crisis and political tensions in Venezuela led many US analysts to believe that the Venezuelan regime was extremely fragile, and on the verge of collapse. It was reasoned that with just a little more pressure, the regime would tumble like a house of cards, paving the way for the return of normal democracy. Certainly, top advisers to President Trump convinced him of this. It was felt that isolating the regime diplomatically, applying economic sanctions, and encouraging the people to rise up in rebellion would tip the scales. This had worked against authoritarian regimes like Ferdinand Marcos of the Philippines, Slobodan Milosevic and others. However, to the dismay of the international community the regime of Nicolas Maduro not only remained in power, but appeared to be stronger as of this writing (October 2019) than it did in January 2019.

Why? Because although Venezuela can be stressed, it is not subject to the same stresses that conventional states are subject to. In particular, the regime is no longer vitally dependent on the legal economy. Rather, over the last ten years, it has systematically diversified and switched its major sources of revenue to drug trafficking, money laundering and illegal mining. As a result, diplomatic and economic isolation have impact, but not much to the survival of the regime. As long as these sources remain intact, the regime can weather the storm as long as the West fails to take a radically different approach.

A different approach is badly needed. However, the new forms of conflict have been difficult concepts for many in the United States institutions to grasp. As Maslow pointed out in his 1966 law of the instrument "when all you have is a hammer, everything looks like a nail." Even more so when that hammer (our military establishment) has cost several hundred billion dollars to build and maintain. We have vested so much money, time, energy, education and training into creating our fantastic hammer that to claim that our main tool is no longer optimal for the problems we face, does not cognitively compute. We keep on trying to make our enemies become nails, rather than modifying our tools to combat the true nature of the problem.

How do you apply military force when your enemy's main form of combat is criminally financed social protest? How do you apply this tool when the main form of combat is money laundering disguised behind a façade of corruption? Or, how do you send an Airborne Division to confront striking teachers? It is not fair to say that our system is unaware of what is going on, but so far, we seem to want to make only slight adjustments to our "hammer" rather than to develop completely new or perhaps more flexible tools to combat these new forms of conflict. Perhaps the problem is not so much awareness as the great difficulty of making quick and radical direction changes to huge bureaucratic and legalistic institutions. Democratic institutions are designed this way, to avoid being subjected to every political whim of the moment, but in this case, this design characteristic is ceding great maneuver space to our rivals.

Can we design new, flexible and agile tools and maintain the essence of our democracy?

While I cannot hope to develop a viable solution in the brief space of this article, I do think that the first step is better awareness. Our intelligence and security agencies have been too slow to pick up on these trends. While there are very intelligent analysts within the community, and much excellent work is being done, there is too much group think and too many rewards for being politically correct rather than for critical thinking. The intelligence failures that led to September 11, 2001 and the absence of significant weapons of mass destruction in Iraq are only the most public examples, but there have been many other intelligence failures with lesser, and thus not public, consequences to date because of this type of thinking.

Too few intelligence analysts speak the language of the countries they are analyzing. For example, it is unconscionable that in a country where 17.6% of the population are Hispanics and 17% of the military are Hispanic, that most intelligence officer dealing with Latin America are not fluent Spanish speakers. Additionally, for all the Ivy League graduates in the Intelligence community, few have spent their lives and careers focused enough on a single issue to the point where they become true subject matter experts. Being a generalist is more valued and rewarded than being a specialist. This is hurting our ability to develop a deep understanding of what's going on which is more critical today than ever before. Finally, Intelligence is sometimes blocked from being passed forward to the decision-makers because it is considered politically sensitive or controversial. Bad news or different thinking is often not rewarded, so rather than present it as alternative thinking, it is suppressed. It seems to me that intelligence should not be subject to these kinds of filters until they reach the decision-makers themselves. The decision-maker can then weight and value the intelligence and use his own criteria to make the political decision. After all, that's what he's being paid for.

The Convenience of Convergence between Terrorism and Organized Crime: When a Haram becomes a Halal

Leonardo Coutinho

Leonardo Coutinho is an expert on transnational threats in Latin America, specializing in corruption, drug trafficking, and transnational crime. Coutinho has provided briefings to universities and policy makers in South America and United States on international terrorism hubs in Brazil, the Venezuela crisis, and corruption cases and investigations He has testified before both the US Congress and the Brazilian Congress.

Coutinho is the author of the book "Hugo Chávez, o espectro" published in Portuguese in 2018, and a coauthor of the book "Iran's Strategic Penetration of Latin America", published by Lexington Books in October 2014. In March 2019, he released a chapter of the book "Perspectivas do Terrorismo Transnacional Contemporâneo". Coutinho currently serves as the International Fellow from Brazil for the next generation, national security think tank Center for a Secure Free Society (SFS), based in Washington D.C. Prior to SFS, Mr. Coutinho was a journalist for VEJA magazine, where he published several investigations about Iran´s activities in Latin America and extremists' cells in Brazil and other countries. He is a six-time winner of the Journalist Award from Grupo Abril.

This text is an adapted version of: Leonardo Coutinho. "TERRORISMO E CRIME ORGANIZADO: A EMERGÊNCIA DAS AMEAÇAS HÍBRIDAS" published originally in: Carlos Frederico Felício Fagundes, Jorge Mascarenhas Lasmar e José Fernando Moraes Chuy (Orgs). Perspectivas do Terrorismo Transnacional Contemporâneo. Ed Arraes. Brazil (March 2019)

"We produce drugs for Satan, which are the United States and the Jews.

If we cannot kill them with weapons, we will kill them with drugs."

–Muhammad Hussein Fadlallah

1979 was a singular year. China opened its economy and began its journey towards the quiet conquest of the West. Chinese leader Deng Xiaoping became the first Chinese Head of State to visit Washington since the communist revolution thirty years earlier. The agreements reached and signed during that visit were the starting point for transforming the economic matrix of an eminently agricultural country that in just a few decades would establish itself as the second largest economy in the planet.

In the same year of 1979, in the Middle East, Sunnis and Shiites experienced radical changes of their political and religious relations. In Iran, the Islamic Revolution headed by Ayatollah Ruhollah Khomeini (1902-1989) led this country to a position of permanent antagonism with the West and especially with its foremost representative, the United States. The rise of the Shiite theocracy in Iran was marked by violence. Nearly 300 Shia radicals stormed the Great Mosque of Mecca and killed almost two hundred Muslim faithful in pilgrimage to the sacred city of Islam. This event marked a hardening of the two sides of Islam, just at the same time as religion was embracing politics as an element of protest, struggle and radicalization.

By the end of 1979 the Union of Soviet Socialist Republics (USSR) invaded Afghanistan, of Sunni majority, which caused a reaction hitherto unheard of: the rise of jihadism.

Thus, under the argument of the defense of religion against the infidels, political Islam found in fundamentalism the fertile ground to promote and develop terrorism, which in turn would reach new levels of lethality.

Although at first sight they seem to be isolated from each other, the events of 1979 are the starting point for conflicts that have become endless and that inexorably redefined the war models as we used to know them.

The succession of events derived from these milestones and the history of terrorism itself can be seen as an evolutionary process, although surely it was also the result of knowledge transfer and learning.

In modern terrorism there are no boundaries between terrorist organizations and those of the transnational organized crime. Drug trafficking, which is in the genesis of the utterly devastating wave of violence sweeping today most Latin American countries, especially Mexico and the so-called Northern Triangle (El Salvador, Guatemala and Honduras), is at the epicenter of this strategic union. In Brazil — the country in which most homicides are directly linked one way or another to drug trafficking — the situation is not different.[40] According to official data on violent deaths, 63,880 were killed in Brazil in 2017 alone.[41]

Scholars who specialize in terrorism often divide this type of organizations into four waves, the third of which is the one that mostly comprised the armed groups of the ideological left. It was precisely this wave that marked indelibly with fire several countries in Latin America. It was here that cocaine trafficking flourished as the most important source for the financing of armed

---

[40] SAPORI, Luís Flávio; SOARES, *Gláucio Ary Dillon. Por que cresce a violência no Brasil?* Belo Horizonte: Autêntica Editora/Editora PUC Minas, 2014.

[41] FÓRUM BRASILEIRO DE SEGURANÇA PÚBLICA. Anuário Brasileiro de Segurança Pública 2018. Segurança Pública em números.

organizations. In Peru, the Shining Path terrorists received up to 95% of their income from cocaine trafficking.[42] Created in the 70s, this Maoist organization was responsible for more than 31,000 deaths in the years that followed, the 80s being the deadliest of all.

During those years, Shining Path terrorists were only surpassed in their degree of lethality by the Colombian FARC (Revolutionary Armed Forces of Colombia), which is the terrorist organization with the deadliest record and most extensive lists of victims in the history of the West.[43]

Just like Shining Path, the FARC cashed in — and still does — on drug trafficking as its main source of income, followed by cattle rustling, kidnapping and extortions.

The financial success of the Latin American organizations inspired older terrorist groups, born out of the anti-colonial struggle (defined as the second wave), to imitate their method and seek in drug trafficking their own source of support and survival. Operations against cocaine trafficking carried out by the Brazilian Federal Police, found out for the first time a link between narcotics traffickers and terrorist organizations from the Middle East.

In 1992, Walled Issa Khamays, a Jordanian citizen, was arrested in Brazil while trying to ship 595 kilos of cocaine to Europe.[44]

The investigations that led to the arrest of Khamays made clear that cocaine shipments were intended to fill the coffers of the Palestine

---

[42] BERRY, LaVerle et al. "A global overview of narcotics-funded terrorist and other extremist groups". A report prepared by the Federal Research Division, Library of Congress under an Interagency Agreement with the Department of Defense, May 2002

[43] Deutsche Welle, "Conflito armado deixou mais de 260 mil mortos na Colômbia, diz relatório." *Globo.* August 2, 2018. Available at: https://g1.globo.com/mundo/noticia/2018/08/02/conflito-armado-deixou-mais-de-260-mil-mortos-na-colombia-diz-relatorio.ghtml

[44] LUCCHELLI, Giuseppe. "Il Vero Killer? Detenuto in un AltroPaese". *La Repubblica*, Roma,02/09/1992.

Liberation Front (FPLP).[45] The operation, during which the Palestinian operatives were caught red-handed, wasn't the first under Khamays' supervision and coordination. That same year he had already sent another 325 kilos of cocaine to Europe.

Khamays activities became the clearest evidence to date of a terrorist organization, born and raised during the so-called "anti-colonial wave", resorting to cocaine trafficking as a source of financing and logistical supply — until then, a pattern limited to the leftist armed groups.

His arrest and the subsequent exposure of his links to terrorism must have had the impact of a "black swan" event in regard to the analysis of the implications of Islamic terrorism-drug trafficking hybridization,[46] something deemed unlikely vis-à-vis the rules of this religion, but that nonetheless existed, although it was barely known.

The exert introducing this text is not a tribute:

> "We produce drugs for Satan, which are the United States and the Jews.
>
> If we cannot kill them with weapons, we will kill them with drugs." [47]

It is actually part of a fatwa — an opinion in the Koranic law that generates jurisprudential effect as it is an interpretation that modifies the application of the rules of Shariah [48] (Islamic Law) to

---

[45] EMBARGOS de Declaração na Extradição 936 –República Italiana. In: Revista Trimestral de Jurisprudência, Supremo Tribunal Federal, v. 196, n. 3, p. 744-751, April/June 2006.

[46] TALEB, Nassim Nicholas. *The Black Swan: The impact the highly improbable.* New York: Random House, 2007.

[47] LEVITT, Matthew. Hizbullah narco-terrorism: a growing cross-border threat. IHS Defence, Risk and Security Consulting, Washington, D.C., 2012.

[48] Shariah is the set of laws and precepts that govern Muslim behavior and civil and criminal law in Islamic countries. It is defined as the Koranic law, therefore,

justify an activity banned by Islam, or otherwise regulate it — which reflects in its translation the true spirit of a threat that has generally been ignored.

It is about hybridization between terrorist organizations and organized crime.

Ayatollah Muhammad Hussein Fadlallah (1935-2010), who was the spiritual leader of the Shiite militia known as Hezbollah, issued this decree to allow the use of drug trafficking as an asymmetrical war instrument.[49] For this cleric, as long as the illegal activity was used as a weapon in the battle against the infidels, it ceased to be haram (sin) and became halal (lawful), a decision clearly defined by utter convenience.

This Fatwa was revealed as an extremely important instrument for Hezbollah, since not only did it legitimize drug trafficking from a religious point of view per se, but it also covered it with a justification, giving a mantle of "nobility" to an activity that is definitely criminal.

By giving drug trafficking — especially cocaine from South America — the status of a jihad tool, the organization appeased its

---

divine and immutable. It is not organized in a "criminal code" as is standard for legal norms. Its guidelines are drawn directly from the Islamic holy texts. In Western countries, where Muslim communities are minorities, Islamic jurisprudence undergoes adaptations approved by the Fatwa councils, organizations composed of sheikhs that issue religious advice on issues that can generate conflicts or doubts for the faithful. An example would be to exempt a woman from wearing the hijab so she can access the labor market, or allow a believer to borrow with interests to pay a mortgage, trivial matters of living in society that are affected by religious norms. See more at: OXFORD ISLAMIC STUDIES ONLINE. Available at
http://www.oxfordislamicstudies.com/article/opr/t125/e2168.

[49] LEVITT, op. cit.

critics and managed to turn even its most religious members into traffickers.[50]

Thus, cocaine became an important factor in financing the logistics of Hezbollah's activities. The first evidence of the convergence between Hezbollah's terrorist activities and drug trafficking were identified by the Argentinean officials investigating the attacks against the Israeli embassy in Buenos Aires (1992) — 29 people killed, 242 injured —, and the Israeli Argentinean Mutual Association, (AMIA in Spanish) (1994) - 84 killed, 300 injured.

According to official documents in the dossier of the 1992 attack, it was fully demonstrated that cocaine trafficking activities were directly linked with the logistical operatives of the attack on the embassy.[51] According to what the Argentinean justice stated in a communiqué dated in 1999, several members of the Hezbollah cell embedded in the Triple Frontier area (Argentina, Brazil and Paraguay) were also drug traffickers.[52]

The Argentinean investigators concluded that the attack was coordinated by Imad Fayiz Mughniyah (1962-2008), commander of Hezbollah in charge of the organization's operations abroad.

The judicial document states that Mughniyah traveled to the Brazilian city of Foz do Iguaçu to negotiate the purchase of the explosives later used in the attack on the Israeli embassy.

Mughniyah's counterpart was the Syrian national Monzer Al Kassar, who at the time was considered one of the world's most prominent active arms dealers.[53] Al Kassar was also a contact of

---

[50] COUTINHO, op. cit.

[51] COUTINHO, op. cit.

[52] Available at:
http://public.diariojudicial.com/documentos/000/058/054/000058054.pdf

[53] KEEFE, Patrick Radden. "The trafficker: the decades-long battles to catch an international arms broker". *The New Yorker*, February 8, 2010.

the drug trafficking operator in Brazil for the Palestine Liberation Front, the Jordanian citizen Walled Issa Khamays.

This sequence of events should be enough evidence that despite being expressly prohibited by the sacred texts of Islam, drug trafficking was and is a reality inherent to insurgency and terrorism operations carried out by Islamic radical organizations.

This is based on a "moral" justification derived from the perception that, if it is used as part of the asymmetrical war strategy at the service of jihad, drug trafficking is not only allowed but also encouraged.

The adaptive capacities of terrorist and organized crime organizations thus became a challenge for security and defense institutions throughout the world. The evolution of terrorism over decades, as well as the mutation of transnational criminal organizations, demonstrate that their leaders and members have been able to adapt and adjust the modus operandi of their activities and make them complementary, taking advantage of their strengths and correcting their weaknesses.

More than a purely conceptual evolution, terrorists have been able to perceive and develop their adaptive capacities.

In fact, since these organizations are not governed by ethical and moral values, and they are not subject to institutional rules, as is the case with the conventional armed and police forces, the convergence between terrorism and drug trafficking goes on unrestricted.

Various investigations conducted in Brazil in the last two decades are an obvious sign that the country has become an important laboratory for the convergence between Islamic terror and drug trafficking.

In 2006, the United States' Department of the Treasury released its first list of Lebanese and Brazilian citizens living in the Triple Frontier region who are accused of having links with Hezbollah.[54]

According to the US authorities, important terrorist financing networks operated in the cities of Foz do Iguaçu (Brazil) and Ciudad del Este (Paraguay). The measure included individual sanctions and penalties against companies registered to the names of operatives of the Lebanon-based Shiite organization.

One of the names exposed by the United States was Farouk Abdul Omairi's. This businessman had been identified as one of the main Hezbollah operatives in Brazil. That same year, Omairi was arrested in Brazil, accused of being the head of the cocaine trafficking operations. He was one of the main targets of the so-called "Operation Camelo."[55]

Still, although the country's Federal Police had enough evidence to confirm the activities of Islamic extremists in Brazil, they could only be charged for crimes of a milder nature, due to the absence of a law against terrorism that would only be passed in 2016.[56]

Condemned for cocaine trafficking in Brazil and accused by the United States of being the head of Hezbollah's financial operations on the Triple Frontier, Omairi was the clearest and most obvious link between the Shiite militia and organized crime.[57]He had under

---

[54] TREASURY TARGETS Hezbollah Fundraising network in the triple frontier of Argentina, Brazil, and Paraguay. U.S Department of the Treasury, Washington (DC), 12/06/2006.

[55] PRESÍDIO FEDERAL DE MS recebe suspeitos de integrar Hezbollah. G1, January 24 2008.

[56] COUTINHO, Leonardo. "Turning the tables: how Brazil defeated an ISIS threat". *Global Dispatch*, Center for a Secure Free Society, Washington, D.C., issue 5, September 2017

[57] LEALI, Francisco. "Polícia federal aponta elo entre facção brasileira e Hezbollah". *O Globo*, 9 de November de 2014.

his control a complex network, deeply rooted within the Muslim communities in the Triple Frontier, Curitiba and Sao Paulo.

Reports indicate that he was involved in the coordination and issuance of false documents, as well as in money laundering. drug trafficking, however, was the main source of the resources generated by Omairi, kind of a Hezbollah CEO for the region.

Until he began operations in South America, Hezbollah was limited to acting as a drug trafficking intermediary in Lebanon and some parts of Israel. In 1984, the Journal of Palestine Studies published the trade balance data between the two neighboring countries. It showed that the underground or "black" economy, coordinated by the Shiites, was the main exchange activity between Lebanon and Israel. That year, the Lebanese sent across the border an estimated 700 tons of hashish and a ton and a half of heroin, opium and liquid hashish.[58]

Yet Omairi is not the only name on the list of individuals convicted by the United States Department of Justice with proven links to cocaine trafficking. Investigations carried out by the Brazilian Federal Police brought to jail important members of clans reported as sponsors and operatives of Hezbollah in the Triple Frontier.[59]

Likewise, the investigations conducted by Argentinean federal prosecutors on the attack against the headquarters of the AMIA, in 1994, left no doubt. The Brazilian cell had been the source of funding for the attack against the Jewish institution in Buenos Aires.[60]

---

[58] COUTINHO, 2018a.

[59] OTTOLENGHI, Emanuele. "Examining the effectiveness of Kingpin Designation Act in the Western Hemisphere". Foundation for Defense of Democracies, November 8, 2017

[60] COUTINHO, Leonardo. "Iran and Hezbollah in the Western Hemisphere": statement before the US House of Representatives Committee on Foreign Affairs Subcommittee on the Western Hemisphere & Subcommittee on the Middle East and North Africa. Washington (DC), Serial number 114-34, 03/18/2015a. p. 76-81.

The emergence of a full-fledged "Shiite Cartel" in Brazil was not the only example to illustrate the convergence between Islamic extremists and cocaine trafficking as a source of funds for terrorist activities.

In the early 2000s, as soon as Hugo Chávez's first term as president of Venezuela began, the then dictator of Cuba, Fidel Castro, met with his Venezuelan pupil in Caracas. During that meeting, Chávez expressed his willingness to support the FARC, so that they could resist the impact of the recently implemented Plan Colombia and how it would inevitably affect their main source of financial income. The FARC knew, as well as Chávez and Fidel, that the military program, which included spraying defoliants over the coca plantations, would lead to the collapse of the narcotics production, a fact that indeed would take place twelve years later.[61]

At the aforementioned meeting, Chávez said to his Cuban counterpart that, from an ideological point of view, he had already decided to support the FARC terrorists. However, he had a problem with their drug trafficking.

As witnesses of the meeting point out, Fidel Castro then gave Chávez a lecture on pragmatism and "revolutionary" strategy.[62] Castro explained that cocaine was no real problem at all; on the contrary, cocaine was an instrument in the struggle against imperialism.

Using his didactic ways, the Cuban dictator convinced Chávez that, by offering his full and unrestricted support to the FARC, he would not only be promoting the revolution in the neighboring country but also causing damage to the United States. The increase in drug trafficking, Fidel taught him, would force the Americans to spend more money on law enforcement actions, as well as on the treatment of addicts.

---

[61] COUTINHO, Leonardo. "Os gigolôs da paz". *Veja*, January 31 2018.

[62] COUTINHO, 2018a.

Chavez not only opened the doors of Venezuela to the FARC's drug trafficking operations, but in fact he committed his military to provide logistical support. Using the Armed Forces for drug trafficking purposes was the beginning of the criminalization process of the Venezuelan State and accelerated the erosion of the country's institutions. Members of the military high command became rich with these operations and gave rise to the so-called "Cartel de los Soles".[63] In short, what was originally supposed to be just an ideological support operation ended with the whole government structure hooked up and dependent on illegal activities.

According to testimonies of former members of the high echelons of Chavismo, cocaine trafficking became so tolerable for local commanders that it practically became "official."[64]

In 2015, US law enforcement, in a joint operation with Haitian authorities, caught red-handed two nephews of Venezuelan President Nicolas Maduro.[65] These individuals were directly involved in a scheme to send 800 kilos of cocaine to Mexican cartels. The final destination of the drug would be the United States.

The investigations revealed that the money obtained by such drug trafficking was destined to cover electoral campaign expenses for the leaders of the Chavista regime.

Four years earlier, the world discovered that another barrier between drug trafficking and terrorism had fallen, and the tentacles of these mixed operations were no longer limited. In October 2011

---

[63] NUEVAS DENUNCIAS para el gobierno de Chávez. "El poder judicial venezolano está penetrado por el narcotráfico". *El Imparcial*, América, September 21, 2018.

[64] Ludmila Vinogradoff, "Cabello: EE.UU. podría invadir Venezuela, su problema será salir," ABC, July 29, 2019. Available at: https://www.abc.es/internacional/abci-cabello-eeuu-podria-invadir-venezuela-problema-sera-salir-201907290240_noticia.html

[65] COUTINHO, Leonardo. "Cai a fronteira entre o regime venezuelano e o narcotráfico". *Veja*, 13 November 2015.

the United States discovered a plan to carry out an attack in Washington DC. The ayatollahs of Iran, the terrorists of Hezbollah and the drug traffickers of the Mexican Cartel Los Zetas established a Joint Venture to kill Adel Al Jubeir, at the time the Saudi Arabian ambassador, by perpetrating a bomb attack against him right there in the capital city of the United States.[66]

In Brazil, the redundancy of drug trafficking investigations identifying targets suspected of links to Islamic terrorism has become an alert that the collusion of these activities has a tremendous destructive potential for public security. One of the most sophisticated and best structured criminal organizations in Brazil, the Primeiro Comando da Capital (PCC), which operates in conjunction with criminal organizations in Bolivia, Paraguay and Argentina, is pointed out by a number of investigators as the strategic and logistic partner of Hezbollah in international operations designed for Africa, Europe and the Middle East.

The evolution of the PCC as a criminal organization would be directly linked to the fact that one of its leaders had shared a prison cell with a Chilean terrorist educated and trained by some of the most recognized organizations of the Latin American armed left.[67]

Their organizational models, the methods of negotiation and the "kidnapping" of the State through violent actions are typical of the insurgency strategy adopted by those groups.

International terrorist organizations, especially Hezbollah, have a huge "capital" to offer to criminal organizations in exchange for

---

[66] DEPARTMENT OF JUSTICE. Office of Public Affairs. Manssor Arbabsiar Sentenced in New York City Federal Court to 25 Years in Prison for Conspiring with Iranian Military Officials to Assassinate the Saudi Arabian Ambassador to the United States. May 30, 2013. Available at:
http://www.justice.gov/opa/pr/manssor-arbabsiar-sentenced-new-york-city-federal-court-25-years-prisonconspiring-iranian.

[67] CHRISTINO, Marcio Sergio; TOGNOLLI, Claudio. *Laços de sangue: a história secreta do PCC*. São Paulo: Matrix Editora, 2017

access to cocaine, their local logistics and their ability to send huge financial resources to the international markets. In other words, in exchange for this access, Hezbollah makes available to its allies its powerful money laundering network and its "legal" ways of justifying or, if necessary, hiding the flow of millions of dollars.

An expertise consolidated after decades participating in merchandise trade, as well as in smuggling, perfected by the vital need to cover up its military operations against local targets and in the West.

For many years, that alliance was treated as something unthinkable or as the fruit of conspiracy theories. Unfortunately, an overview of the joint operations by these groups clearly shows that they do not follow a predictable logic and that the waging of "unbounded wars,"[68] both by terrorism and organized crime, is a reality that demands a new way to counter them, and innovate the concepts of security and defense.

In modern conflicts there are no longer restrictions for the forms of struggle to be employed.[69] Organized crime and terrorism no longer entertain any impediment to the viability of their goals.

---

[68] LIANG, Qiao e XIANGSUI, Wang. *Unrestricted Warfare*. Beijing. PLA Literature and Arts Publishing House. February 1999. Available at: http://www.c4i.org/unrestricted.pdf

[69] LIANG and XIANSUI, 1999. The multiple forms of fighting, according to Qiao Liang and Wang Xiangsui, include military and non-military elements although they all compete for the same goal. For them, these ingredients can be: "atomic war, diplomatic war, financial war, conventional war, commercial war, biochemical war, intelligence war, resource war, ecological war, psychological war, economic war, space war, tactical war, regulatory warfare, electronic warfare, smuggling warfare, sanction warfare, guerrilla warfare, drug warfare (drug trafficking), media warfare, terror warfare (terrorism), virtual warfare (deterrence), ideological warfare." For them, none of these modalities necessarily has to be adopted separately. They can be combined with each other "giving rise to a new model." The literal transcription has the purpose of showing how in the

The alliance between the PCC and Hezbollah has deepened and today they work together in drug and arms trafficking. According to investigations by Brazil's Federal Police, Hezbollah sells weapons to Brazilian criminal organizations using the PCC's connections and services in Brazil, and simultaneously using their logistics networks from the borders of Paraguay and Bolivia, to the ports of the Brazilian coast. Hezbollah has also mediated in the sale of C4 plastic explosive stolen in Paraguay and sold on the black market at very low prices.[70]

In permanent conflict with the West since 1979, Iran teaches that to achieve its strategic objectives not even the essence of its theocracy, the Sharia law itself, must be an obstacle. Its alliance through Hezbollah with organizations such as the Mexican Zetas, the coca growers of Bolivia, the PCC in Brazil, demonstrates that for the regime of the Ayatollahs, even the most rigid rules are abandoned in the name of undertaking efficient actions against the enemy.

What is illegal or lawful (Haram or Halal) according to the Islamic faith, gains enormous flexibility when the fact of the matter is to achieve victory over the enemy; that is, those most conveniently defined as "the infidels."

---

authors' conception "war" is the central word, and therefore incessantly repeated. But "war," as they point out, should not be read as regular or conventional conflict. An army against another army type of war. The authors propose a new generation of "war", using traditional models, but especially asymmetric or irregular ones.

[70] LEALI, Francisco. "Polícia Federal aponta elo entre facção brasileira e Hezbollah (Federal Police link Brazilian faction and Hezbollah)," *O Globo*, November 9, 2014. Available at: http://oglobo.globo.com/brasil/policiafederalaponta-elo-entre-faccao-bra-sileira-hezbollah-14512269

Cuba: The Unforeseen Transition From Communism to a Mafia State

Juan Antonio Blanco, PhD

Juan A. Blanco is currently the Executive Director of the Foundation for Human Rights in Cuba.

Juan A. Blanco holds a PhD in History of International Relations from the University of Havana where he worked as a university professor. Later on he served as a diplomat in Cuba's Ministry of Foreign Affairs and as as senior analyst of US- Cuba relations for the Communist Party of Cuba Central Committee's Department of the Americas. After his defection in Canada, he became the Director for Latin American programs at Human Rights Internet, an international NGO based in Ottawa. In the United States he worked as Visitor Director at the Cuban Research Institute of Florida International University, and later on as Executive Director of the Center for Latin American and Caribbean Initiatives at Miami Dade College. For more than two decades, has been actively participating in multiple initiatives of the Cuban exile community in Canada and Miami.

As an international analyst of Cuba's foreign policy, Mr. Blanco has been invited to make presentations at prestigious universities and think-tanks in the United States and Europe. He is regularly invited to participate in TV and radio shows on Cuba and other international relations topics. He is author of several books and essays about conflict management, Cuban transition, diasporas and development, character assassination, and geopolitics.

SUMMARY

Mafia State is a category coined by some political scientists to analyze a recent phenomenon in international relations. It is not another pejorative expression to refer to autocratic or totalitarian States.

A new Mafia State may emerge wherever an autocratic political elite that ends up dominating State institutions and controlling national policies, use them to run criminal operations for their own benefit while keeping their activities beyond the reach of any national institutional check and balances or international monitoring.

After the fall of the USSR and having lost the geopolitical ecosystem that sustained it for more than three decades, the emergence of the alliance with Hugo Chavez and his kleptocratic power elite in an oil rich country as Venezuela opened the door to what then was an unforeseen transition possibility for Cuba. Instead of moving towards a liberal open society with a market economy, the collusion of the ruling elites of both countries made possible a Cuban a different kind of transition: from communism into a Mafia State. Cubazuela was born.

A transition and transformation from a repressive communist society into a Mafia State structurally alters, among other factors, the composition of the ruling elite, the allocation of power, the sources and mechanisms for the appropriation of wealth and privilege, and the culture of domination used by the ruling group. It also implies a dramatic change in the selection and roles of external allies and in the methods to wage asymmetric, hybrid conflict with enemies.

These new species cannot be approach as if they were Westphalian behaved states. A new vision of the problem is needed — a renewed Weltanschauung in international relations — to understand the true meaning of the emergence of the first transnational Mafia State in Latin America. It is time to change eyeglasses.

From Great Scam to Great Mutation

La Gran Estafa (Mexico 1952)[71] is a mandatory book. In this volume, the outstanding Latin American communist leader Eudocio Ravines denounced for the first time Moscow's true intentions while it justified its policies of interference under a mantle of humanism.

In the Foreword to that first edition, Ravines affirms the following: "It is a scam not to those who believe in the bliss of capitalism: it is a scam to us, who do believe in the redemption of man, who have fought for the liberation of the oppressed, who have endured hunger, persecution, torture, prison (...) for pushing socialism ahead".

Ravines wanted to forewarn about the fact that the humanist doctrine to which he had devoted his life was nothing but a totalitarian, inhuman and imperial project in disguise.

Many Cubans who fought against dictator Fulgencio Batista in order to establish a democracy made similar warnings when that process took a definite turn towards communism. But still the Cuban communist dictatorship that was installed after its fall managed to appear before the world, especially in Latin America, as the expression of a revolutionary, left-wing, progressive, and even humanist movement.

In 1989, the fall of the Berlin Wall coincided with the protests and subsequent massacre in Tiananmen Square, and with the drug trafficking scandal in Cuba. On that occasion, Fidel Castro called to "wash off the offense with blood". Thus, he covered his intention of burying, along with the bodies of those shot by firing squad, the

---

[71] Eudocio Ravines, *La Gran Estafa*, Libros y Revistas S.A: Mexico, 1952

evidence of a mutation that had begun long before.[72] After the earthquake-like commotion of that year, only the genuinely naive or the worse opportunists continued to extend their unconditional support to Havana in the wake of the hasty executions of senior Cuban officers, including General Arnaldo Ochoa.[73]

But these followers of the Cuban process were shaken not only by fear of the consequences of countering the official version, but also by the sense of loss caused when the facts clash against all the beliefs and loyalties of a lifetime. It was what psychologists would call a crisis of cognitive dissonance.[74]

From time to time the communist movement has gone through crises in which it has lost sheep that got tired of being such — as was the case with the repudiation of Stalin's crimes — but it has almost always been able to keep most of the flock appeased. **This was the**

---

[72] José A. Friedl Zapata, *El Gran Engaño*, Santiago Apóstol: Buenos Aires, 2005.

[73] Arnaldo Ochoa. The Cuban general who received most decorations from his own country and from others he served. He was declared a "Hero of the Republic of Cuba" and was a member of the Central Committee of the Communist Party. On August 26, 1958 he joined the guerrilla fight against dictator Fulgencio Batista. In April 1961 he fought at Bay of Pigs. In October 1962 he had a remarkable participation in the Caribbean Missile Crisis. In the 1960's he trained with Venezuelans in Cuba. In July 1966 he landed in Venezuela on Falcon state. In that country he participated in an ambush on Cerro Atascadero on September 16th, 1966 between Yumare and Duaca (Yaracuy State), where they killed an officer, a noncommissioned officer and wounded two soldiers. On February 25th, 1967 he commanded the column that participated in El Mortero ambush, between Sanare and El Blanquito (Lara state), against members of the Venezuelan Army, where they killed three troops and wounded eight. After his return from Venezuela, he was appointed deputy chief of the General Staff. Later he was appointed head of the Military Constructions and the Western Army of Cuba. In 1977, Arnaldo Ochoa was the head of the multinational operation against the Somali incursion in the so-called Ogaden War. In the 1980's, he headed the Cuban Military Mission in Angola.

[74] To think one thing and do the opposite, to say something and act differently: The tension many Cubans experienced could be described as *cognitive dissonance*.

case in Cuba when in 1989 Fidel Castro shot without mercy and in great haste those who could expose his personal complicity with the Cuban drug trafficking operations. He was aware by then that this was known by the CIA, the FBI, the DEA and the federal courts of the United States. After General Ochoa and another three high officers were executed, Washington assumed that Castro had finally learned the dangers associated with these activities and would subsequently modify his behavior. Time proved this assessment wrong.

It is true that Chavez's rise to power allowed Castro to acquire a new source of subsidies and oil. But it also provided him with an alternative to reduce the risks from a reprisal by the United States, by transferring to the territory of another State, his dangerous drug trafficking covert activities and his cooperation with terrorist forces, such as ETA, FARC, ELN and Hezbollah.

The oil that Chávez contributed to consolidate that alliance was obtained by Castro in exchange for assets of strategic value for the now rising new power elite in Venezuela: a model of totalitarian repression along with its expert operators, a vast international network of criminals and terrorists, and agents of influence planted in social movements, media outlets, academic, and political institutions in many countries, not excluding the United States.

But to ensure that Venezuelan employees of this novel criminal outsourcing did not eventually intend to appropriate the logistic networks and contacts provided by the Cubans, Castro undertook the colonization of Venezuela under the banner of revolutionary internationalism. A strategy that has generated a substantive change in the nature of both nations.

Mafia States and their international alliances

While in the 1970s and 80s the Castroist State developed a punctual link with drug trafficking and other illegal operations, after the fall of the USSR and the rise of Chávez to power, the Cuban State suffered an essential mutation in its DNA. **The merging of the dictatorial oligarchies in Cuba and Venezuela gave rise to Cubazuela,[75] the first transnational Mafia State in the Americas.**

Why is it so important for Cuba to maintain its control over Venezuela?

Cuba's colonialist control over Venezuela allows the Cuban government:

a) To implant an extractive parasitic economy on the natural resources of that country in order to ensure its own energy security, while paying back by exporting Cuban professionals as slave labor (whose salaries are appropriated by up to 80%) as well as police and military advisors and systems for repression and control of the population.

b) To use the Venezuelan territory as a platform to launch from afar covert criminal activities (drug trafficking, training of terrorist groups, money laundering and others) that would compromise Cuba's national security if carried out continuously and massively from its own territory.

c) To use Venezuela as an outer defense perimeter of the Cuban power elite, by making use of its porous borders with several South American and Caribbean countries, in order

---

[75] Juan Antonio Blanco, Rolando Cartaya, Luis Domínguez, Casto Ocando. *Cubazuela, chronicle of a Cuban intervention*. FHRC, Foundation for Human Rights in Cuba: Miami, 2019. Available at: https://www.fhrcuba.org/2019/04/cubazuela-chronicle-of-a-cuban-intervention/

to implement a model of asymmetric warfare far from its national territory.

This time, it was not about the resurgence of communism, but the birth of an unknown species, not registered until then by the taxonomists of political science: the Mafia State.[76] This new species is not comparable to those States in which significant groups of politicians associate with criminal organizations and favor them with various privileges.

Mafia States may emerge when an autocratic political elite dominating State institutions and controlling national policies, use them to run criminal operations for their own benefit while keeping their activities beyond the reach of any national institutional check and balances or international monitoring.

We are no longer dealing with governments in which some corrupt officials collaborate with criminal elements, but a situation in which the entire government, the State itself, is now controlled by criminal minded elites who transform it into an institution at their service.[77]

The Sao Paulo Forum and ALBA were not thought of by Castro as a new leftist, communist or revolutionary international. Those

---

[76] For an analysis of Mafia States See:
Moisés Naím, "Mafia States. Organized Crime Takes Office". *Foreign Affairs*, May / June 2012. Available at:
https://www.foreignaffairs.com/articles/2012-04-20/mafia-states

Maria Snegovaya, "The Implications of Russia's Mafia State". American Interest. *The American Interest*. December 23rd, 2015. Available at:
https://www.the-american-interest.com/2015/12/23/the-implications-of-russias-mafia-state/

Bálint Magyar, *The Post- Communist Mafia State, The Case of Hungary*, Central European University & Noran Libro Kiadó: Hungary, 2016

[77] According to Moisés Naím, (the mafia States) are not just countries where corruption prevails or where organized crime controls important economic activities and even entire regions. See "Estados mafiosos", *El País*, May 5, 2012. Available at:
https://elpais.com/internacional/2012/05/05/actualidad/1336245036_975620.html

were the necessary appearances to catch well-intentioned, unsuspecting, individuals behind whom to hide the criminal intentions of a group of statesmen and politicians and provide a politically respectful umbrella to integrate irregular non-state players such as the narcoterrorists of FARC. Actually, with this this coalition Castro and Chavez were actually aiming at subtlety establishing an international cover up for regional narcoterrorism.[78] According to the new mafia dialectics, solidarity is carried out — with briefcases full of petrodollars — by killing inopportune prosecutors, destroying the rule of law, and creating alliances with international drug trafficking and terrorist forces.

The main concern of these mafia States nowadays is not as much the infiltration and intelligence gathering activities carried out by the CIA, as those that they may come from the DEA, whose representatives in Latin America were quickly rejected and expelled by Chavez, Evo Morales and Rafael Correa, supported in turn by social movements and media outlets infiltrated by Havana's agents of influence. The so-called people's war acquired a modality of total asymmetric, hybrid warfare in which social networks, civil society organizations and other actors become targets to be infiltrated and manipulated, in order to stabilize allied regimes, discredit unfriendly politicians or destabilize hostile governments.

Key state institutions in Cuba and Venezuela were expropriated and used for criminal endeavors by what gradually became a transnational mafia power elite. Such institutions are now part of a multinational criminal enterprise that uses them for the benefit of a transnational oligarchy, which pursues, above all, its own purposes, does not submit to any independent or electoral power and does not even attempt to justify its legitimacy with

---

[78] Douglas Farah, *Cuba's role in the Bolivarian populist and radical movement's dismantling of democracy*. Miami: Interamerican Institute for Democracy, 2018

Marxist theories or popular benefits. That merger produced a modern colony whose metropolis is in Havana.

The initial strategy followed by Cuba of partially interfering in Venezuela became an interventionist policy of a neo-colonial nature. The initial political alliance between two radical and anti-American governments to secure Havana's parasitic economy after the fall of the USSR, suffered a genetic mutation.

At the beginning of the new millennium, the power elites of Cuba and Venezuela merged into a transnational criminal enterprise. Its system of alliances and cooperation with other governments, criminal groups and terrorist forces — regional and extra-regional — can be considered the first transnational Narco State anchored in the Western Hemisphere.

Since then we were no longer dealing with an independent and sovereign State that controls its national territory, protects the welfare and security of its citizens, and lives in peace with its neighbors. Key economic and military state institutions in both countries colluded to enable the emergence of a criminal transnational enterprise.

The Venezuelan power elite has handed over national independence to Cuba, which has established there a modern model of colonial domination. It has also ceded territories to foreign criminal groups (FARC, ELN, and Hezbollah) in which laboratories for drug production have been installed.

It's healthy to remind the Marxists, so adept at looking for regularities and even "laws" that dictate the historical evolution, that the emergence of the Mafia State in some post-communist States is not the result of chance. There are historical circumstances to explain it.

Let us return to Ravines and his 1952 Foreword: "I know well that the scam is not a product of the perfidy of an evil leader, or the ambitious cruelty of a clan that owns power. It is the inexorable consequence of systems and methods; of inhuman dogmas that cannot be abandoned; of economic, political and social conditions which the Soviet leaders cannot modify or soften, since that would lead to their fall".

We should have paid more attention to Ravines when he wrote those lines. A certain set of historical circumstances are required for enabling the birth of a Mafia State.

Countries under military conflicts, with failed States, dysfunctional political and justice systems, without a development perspective and with impoverished societies, are breeding grounds conducive to the emergence of criminal activities. Post-communist countries offer that potential because of the DNA of the totalitarian regimes of governance they come from.

In societies without the rule of law, the emergence of various forms of cooperation and even alliances between some criminal politicians and common criminals was a historical necessity. That reality could be made effective in dysfunctional States such as Mexico, some Central America countries, in certain regions such as Sicily, or in entire countries that underwent a regime change from a totalitarian society like the USSR.[79]

---

[79] The critical reaction by Peter Andrea (Carnegie Endowment for Peace), regarding an essay by Moisés Naím (Council for Foreign Relations NY) on the mafia State contains some flaws. It is not valid to equate the phenomena of punctual infiltration of State institutions by the mafia (such as those in Italy) to the full occupation of the State apparatus by a mafia, as is the case today in Venezuela. That is the difference between the criminal penetration of the Colombian State by organized crime at the time of Pablo Escobar and the Venezuelan criminal state in the Chávez era. Andreas, as a historian, remembers rightly that there always throughout history criminal activities that transcended State borders. But that does not grant an intellectual license to confuse that trans territoriality with the dangerous global dimension of the current processes in motion. See: Peter Andreas "Measuring the Mafia-State MenaceAre Government-Backed Gangs a Grave New Threat?" *Foreign Affairs,* July-August 2012. Available at:
https://www.foreignaffairs.com/articles/2012-07-01/measuring-mafia-state-menace

The Leninist doctrine and the communist States had all the necessary ingredients to facilitate over time the change in the DNA of some totalitarian societies into mafia states. While not all totalitarian countries inevitably had to go through that evolution, their nature favored it.

The Great Mutation is facilitated in closed societies, with neither democratic institutions, nor separate powers, rule of law, and political and civil liberties; without market economies, with brutal intelligence and police systems, with the military submitted to a political oligarchy, and where a cult of obedience is installed in favor of a supposed "vanguard", infallible and untouchable, with absolute control of the reins of the country.

In a society where it is openly established that the end justifies the means, it is easier to get rid of any moralistic disgust and decide that the enemy of my enemy — the world of common crime in this case — could be my friend. In fact, it may even become my ally. A convenient code of conduct for Mafia States.

Unforeseen Transition: from Communism to Mafia State

The transition we are witnessing today in Cuba and other post-communist societies is not from totalitarian to liberal States as Francis Fukuyama and transitologists foresaw in the 1990's, but from so-called "Real Socialism" to mafia states. If Eudocio Ravines warned about the Great Scam of communism, today we are facing its Great Mutation.[80]

In order to sell the Great Scam to their own populations and to the world, the communist oligarchies needed to comply with certain

---

[80] Venezuela's Investigative Unit, "Venezuela: A Mafia State?", *In Sight Crime*, May 16th, 2018. Available at:
https://www.insightcrime.org/investigations/venezuela-mafia-state/

requirements of the social pact promised to their citizenry: the bartering of eternal social and economic security in exchange for the abdication of every individual political and civil right. That was the currency of the so-called "real socialism."

This was the case until the fall of the USSR, when the communist oligarchies of some of those countries launched the Great Mutation, which was nothing other than their own strategy of mutating from totalitarian inept bureaucracies into klepto-autocratic oligarchies. But in some countries of real socialism the entrepreneurial incapacity of these elites caused them to go further.

From the initial goal, after the fall of the Berlin Wall and the USSR, of becoming an autocratic class with market economies under their hegemony, they began to resume the practice of their worst criminal abilities and skills — who doubts that the KGB and the G-2 are two of their few efficient institutions? — to reign over mafia States. In a globalized world, that new State modality multiplied their privileges and made them valid in any corner of the planet, which contributed billions in convertible currencies to their personal chests.

The Great Mutation no longer required inefficient bureaucrats and ideologues, but experts in covert operations, intelligence, police, and underworld, unscrupulous, financiers to invest in running it. The new criminal class that emerged from that mutation of the communist DNA was no longer interested in sustaining the economic costs of co-opting the population. Coercion was cheaper.

The Cuban Mafia State

The necessary preconditions that favored the transition from the communist scam to the Mafia State were created by Fidel Castro. His *caudillo* leadership style and his gangster habits and logic, acquired during his time at the University of Havana, imposed a peculiar stamp on Cuban communism. The arbitrary confiscation of private properties started by the Castroist process of 1959, and reproduced ever since then in cyclical fashion throughout the years, established the premises to justify the revolutionary right of kleptomaniac tendencies of those controlling the political power. On the other hand, Cuban communism was not only totalitarian but also *caudillista.* Castro emptied of real power the institutions of the Communist Party and the government, disposed of public funds at will, destroyed the accounting system and its transparency in the management of the national economy, established an opaque bottomless *"Comandante's* Reserve" that he managed as his private bank account. Last but not least, he ordered covert operations aimed at the creation of shell companies posing as foreign private corporations - even banking entities - through front men based abroad. He had no scruples since his time in Sierra Maestra in allying with drug producers such as Crescencio Pérez, whom he made a commander, or with drug lords of the 1970's such as Roberto Suarez and Pablo Escobar. or with American criminal elements such as Robert Vesco. He considered drug trafficking another "revolutionary task" that was necessary to undertake.

However, there are differences between a criminal leader that involves some institutions and operational groups in punctual illegal activities and the integral transformation of a communist society into a Mafia State. Such changes were implemented mostly after Chavez survived a coup d'état at the turn of the century and from then on fully surrendered to Havana

Among them, the following could be highlighted:

1. **The consolidation of an oligarchy parallel to the formal institutions for the exercise of power.** It is *that* center of power — not the formal structures and institutions — where strategic guidelines arise from. The associates to that elite, especially the military, in many cases hold important positions in the government and the Communist Party, but that is secondary.

Being a member of the Politburo is less relevant than belonging to the nucleus of the new military oligarchy around Raúl Castro and his family. This elite of power — made up by less than 0.01% of the population — and their surroundings, are the ones who really decide and rule; the government institutions barely execute and manage what those decide. In this new architecture of real power, who is more powerful today, the dictator's daughter, Mariela Castro, or President Miguel Díaz-Canel?

What escapes most Cuba analysts is that the genuine power structure in Cuba is similar to that of a corporation and shaped as concentric circles. At the very center of power is the Castro family together with its most reliable and closest allies, most of them are military figures. They represent no more than a hundred families in a country of more than 11 million citizens. That is the true power elite that leads this transition from communism into a mafia state. Their unstated ambition is to become part of a global elite with unrestricted wealth and privileges similar to those in Russia or China. The rest of the individuals located in the other concentric circles enjoy different levels of privileges similar to those of the bureaucratic class in communist states. They include about a thousand of military and civilian high officials and their families. Individuals such as the recently appointed –no free elections decided his designation- president Miguel Diaz Canel are nothing more than a CEO for the management of the traditional economy and services. The illicit economy is directly run by the Castro Clan and no one out of that tiny and close power elite is even aware of its dimension and activities. Raul Castro son in law, General Lopez Callejas, is probably the only person even within that restricted circle to really know what is going on.

2. **The privileges enjoyed by the new power elite in the Mafia State are connected to incomes that are not accounted for and allow the enjoyment of privileges at global scale.** If under communism the political hierarchy of the bureaucrat ensured — with no need for holding property rights — the unrestricted enjoyment of all national state-owned resources under the Mafia State is the access to large amounts of convertible currencies what differentiate their social status from the common person. We are not referring to the emergence of the new privileged social class that today already earns incomes well above the national average in certain new self-employment sectors. The current transition to a Mafia State facilitates the surge of a new power elite based as before on loyalty and proximity to the Castro family but that now also looks forward to amassing private accumulation of capital, real estate and privileges of global reach.

The new power elite of the Mafia State wishes to enjoy access to luxury goods and services throughout the world, not to be limited as before to the unrestricted usufruct of the national resorts. They manage private resources to rent luxury yachts and spend vacations in the Mediterranean if they so wish. **They want to transform from the national ruling class to a global privileged elite**. Achieving this aspiration presumes that the basis of the new power would not any longer require the vertical promotion in bureaucratic positions that are match with local privileges, but the accumulation of freely convertible currency. It is also significant that the members of the new power elite no longer intend to hide to enjoy their privileged lives. They now enjoy and allow being photographed with celebrities in exclusive places. Let alone they feel oblige to excuse or justify themselves to an increasingly impoverished population.

3. **Military Capitalism[81] is the regime of governance of the new Cuban Mafia State**. This oligarchy appropriates profitable and dollarized institutions while the traditional bureaucratic nomenclature continues to manage over the disaster of the socialist economy. The population has to choose between working for the State and be paid a pittance; being hired by a joint venture company linked to the military, in which they pay a little more and expropriate 90% of the salary contributed by foreign investors; or undertake some work on their own account, burdened by abusive taxation and without their business having legal recognition.

The privileges enjoyed by the holding GAESA, formally adhered to the Cuban Armed Forces but run in opaque and authoritarian fashion by a son in law of Raúl Castro, General Luis Alberto Rodríguez Lopez-Callejas marks the difference between the formal and the illicit economy. GAESA is not audited by any independent institution such as Controlaría General de la República, Ministerio de Economía or the Asamblea Nacional. Whenever the feel it suits their purpose General Rodriguez Lopez-Callejas is entitled to rip the away from any other institutions without even bothering with excuses. The General was in charged on constructing the Port of Mariel and after declining a contract to that end for around 300 million dollars he broke the deal and signed a new one with the Government of Lula

---

[81] State Military Capitalism, a concept coined by the Cuban writer, intellectual and political analyst Carlos Alberto Montaner, to name the transition from Cuban communism to another regime of oligarchic domination. In the words of Montaner:

Roughly speaking, military State capitalism is based on the idea that Cuba's main sources of wealth are in the country's 2,500 medium and large companies, all protected by the State and mostly run by the military; while the minor service establishments, (restaurants, small pensions, private party clowns and endless minutiae) would provide jobs to the bulk of a population carefully guarded, so that they do not accumulate capital, and thus deprive them of their potential political power.

da Silva for almost a billion that was financed by the central bank of Brazil (BANDES). Strange rational that could only be explained if the Port construction was used as a money laundering scheme. Perhaps the General's last name should be changed from Lopez to Lansky.[82]

4. **Two parallel economies are established, one dollarized and pseudo capitalist in the hands of the Castro Clan, and another, unproductive, left to the traditional bureaucracy**. Thus, the power elite gradually moves from controlling and managing the entire economy to control only the most profitable part; the one that provides the logistics for their criminal operations. The rest of the inefficient State economy is left in the hands of the traditional institutions to be managed by bureaucrats. The members of the former nomenclature — without control over the most productive investments such as tourism, and no longer having a function other than managing over the socialist disaster — are every time less capable to respond to an increasingly impoverished population. The existence of these two parallel state structures contribute to disguise the emergence of the new Mafia State and to provide a misleading sense of "socialist continuity" to the uninformed.

How has this gradual, undeclared transition from the Great Scam to the Great Mutation been reflected on Cuba?

Under the motto of pursuing efficiency and suppressing gratuities, Cuban communism gradually got rid of the expectations associated to the Great Scam.

Without granting any political and civil liberties, nor authorizing private property and a free market, the Cuban communist State announced that it would no longer pursue full employment policies;

---

[82] Carlos Cabrera Pérez, "Luis Alberto Rodríguez López-Calleja: El General más peligroso para Cuba", *Cibercuba.* October 23, 2019. Available at: https://www.cibercuba.com/noticias/2019-10-23-u191143-e42839-s27061-luis-alberto-rodriguez-lopez-calleja-general-peligroso

allowed a highly restricted version of self-employment to tackle with increasing unemployment ("take responsibility for yourself, do not expect the state to feed you"); planned the contraction of the health system — whose doctors, trafficked as slaves, [83] now became a source of income for the elites of the new mafia State; reduced social investment in housing construction, repair and maintenance of the health infrastructure and got rid of any other social oriented investment that, unlike those connected to tourism, did not report a benefit to the pockets of the new power elite in the short or medium term.

In sum, the socialist expectations of enjoying assured employment, housing and food, as well as free health care and education, gradually vanish with the advancement of the Mafia State. The suppression of civil and political rights, nevertheless, remains.

As an example, consider the following data:

In the last seven years, 64 hospitals have been closed in Cuba. The country rapidly loses hospitalization capacity (32% since 2010). And the number of polyclinics has been reduced by 9%. Data from economist Carmelo Mesa-Lago show that the total health personnel dropped by 22% from 2008 to 2016. The number of technicians fell by 54% and nurses by 16%. In 2010 alone, 47,000 employees in that sector were laid off.[84]

The curious feature with public health care is that the export of medical services in conditions of modern slavery — in which 80 to 90% of doctors' salaries are confiscated by the Cuban State — turned over $ 6.4 billion in 2018 (more than 50% of the national income in freely convertible currency) according to public statistics of the Oficina nacional de Informacion y Estadisticas (ONEI),

---

[83] Carlos Sánchez Berzaín, *Castrochavismo*, Interamerican Institute for Democracy:Miami, 2019. pp. 113-115

[84] Roberto Álvarez Quiñones, "Prepotencia Médica". January 31st, 2018. *Diario de Cuba*. Available at:
http://www.diariodecuba.com/cuba/1517403326_37036.html

but far from investing those resources to improve the national health system and infrastructure, only the accelerated deterioration of health services is for all to see.

After 2006, housing construction steadily declined to 22,100 units in 2016. Plans for 2017 and 2018 also fell short. The housing deficit is close to one million units.[85]

What about foodstuff? Cuba still needs to import 80% of its national consumption at a cost of about two billion dollars a year. But while investments in new hotel capacities are a priority for a tourism demand in free fall, the necessary investments to ensure food for the population are postponed.[86]

Those sectors of the population in various countries, to which they continue to sell the Great Scam of a non-existent Cuban revolution, should take note of this historical cycle that began with the fall of the USSR. A non-ideological look at Havana or Caracas should return their false expectations to the harsh realities of Cubazuela, where the promises of the Great Scam of Castro-Chavismo yield way to a reality of famine with repression.

Democracy is a defective system that, nevertheless, allows for improvement and constant change. Communism and mafia states are societies born with the intention of becoming eternal.

---

[85] Carmelo Mesa Lago, "La Vivienda en Cuba Socialista y las Reformas Estructurales", December 20th, 2017, *Cuba Posible*. Available at: https://cubaposible.com/vivienda-cuba-socialismo-reformas/

[86] Pedro Monreal, "La inversión en el agro cubano: entre el "hambre de inversiones" y el desperdicio de estas", El Estado como tal: El Blog de Pedro Monreal sobre Cuba. July 19th, 2019. Available at: https://elestadocomotal.com/2019/07/19/la-inversion-en-el-agro-cubano-entre-el-hambre-de-inversiones-y-el-desperdicio-de-estas/

The threat to international peace and security

Former US ambassador to the United Nations, Nikki Haley, aptly put it at a meeting of the Security Council of that international organization devoted to the relationship between human rights and international security: "In case after case, human rights violations and abuses are not merely the incidental byproduct of conflict. They are the trigger for conflict."

Coexisting with totalitarian, brutally repressive regimes have encouraged their rulers, in more than one occasion, to proactively undermine democratic societies in other countries. Since its emergence in Russia in 1917, most communist states have committed to an aggressive — sometimes overt, most times covert — foreign policy.

Since 1959 Cuba followed suit. Its leaders' vision is that it is impossible to trust, much less peacefully coexist, with their adversaries. The degree of Cuba's confrontational policies varies from country to country. But for a small island with a limited population, Cuba has directly engaged in extraordinarily numerous military conflicts in Central and South America, the Caribbean, Middle East, Africa and Asia. It has also conducted terrorist actions within Europe and the United States.[87]

From Panama to Angola, from Bolivia to Vietnam, Cuban regular or irregular forces, varying from contingents of a few dozens to tens of thousands of combatants, intervened in conflicts developing far away from its shores. They did so either armed with light infantry weapons or with heavy gadgetry that included missiles, bombers, tanks and other assets. Since the early sixties, Castro's

---

[87] An interesting documented review of some early terrorist attempts of Castro within the United States can be found in the book by William B. Brewer *Vendetta*. John Wiley & Sons:USA, 1997.

vision was that the best defense for Cuba was to stir conflicts in distant places or create havoc in other countries to distract the powerful US war machinery. Guevara's motto ("Create two, three, many Vietnams"), is a vision that was not abandoned but readjusted, to open the door to the adoption of asymmetric, hybrid war strategies and tactics.

Cuba, a country that since 1959 never had a self-sustained economy, was able with Soviet support, to develop what in the 1980's was a powerful, first class army in the region. But most important, they also built a first-class intelligence machinery that the CIA had considered third or fourth among the best in the planet. After the fall of the USSR, their new ecosystem of support is to be found in the international networks that integrate state and non-state actors for the pursuit of benefits that result from criminal activities.

The Cuban intelligence apparatus has operated for six decades in various continents, building covert infrastructures and logistic systems, and recruiting local agents among foreign military, academia, teachers, journalists, students, politicians, leaders of social movements, NGO's and unions. Many of their current leaders were trained politically or professionally in Cuban schools. Cuba also developed cooperation, based on mutual benefit, with criminal networks in several continents. They allowed the Cuban power elite to exercise significant influence in those countries but also to build and operate shell companies, traffic with weapons to support their plans and allies, as well as to implement money laundering operations.

Cubans are familiar, and generally successful, with the implementation of interfering and outright intervention activities in different societies and cultural contexts. While Havana demands respect from others, the Castro regime had never thought twice when an opportunity arose to exploit the internal problems of other countries included in its hit list.

Conclusion

1. **The Mafia State is a relatively new category coined and use by some political scientists to analyze recently emerged phenomena in international relations.** It is not a propaganda spin or pejorative expression to refer to old autocratic or totalitarian States. Stalin murdered millions while Putin is a selective serial killer but no less dangerous. The Cold War between blocks with opposing systems was not replaced by peace in international relations. What we experience today is the confrontation between a group of democratic states based on the rule of law, and a coalition of authoritarian and Mafia States allied with criminal irregular forces engaged in drug, arms, human trafficking, and terrorism that provides the necessary income to finance repression in their dictatorial societies.

2. **Some — not all — of the communist regimes evolved into mafia states.** That may happen when their bureaucratic oligarchies become criminal power groups exclusively seeking their own enrichment and abandoning their previous commitments to foster the general welfare of the population while they retained their commitment to exercise unrestricted, unchecked, and eternal political power.

3. **Criminals respond to a different logic than traditional governments.** No one should rule out the possibility of exploring the potential for dialogue or negotiation with some members of the power elites of Cubazuela, but whoever tries that approach should be fully aware of who they intend to negotiate with and what their reasoning logic is. Their paradigm is the use of force and absolute power, not to seek consensus. For them, dialogues and negotiation processes are not opportunities to seek solutions of the type

"we all win"; but a window to gain time, study the divisions among their adversaries and exploit whatever differences they may find there. There is a difference between the methodology use by a SWAT negotiator dealing with a terrorist group with hostages, and the politicians and diplomats parleying with their peers, even if they are adversaries. SWAT obtains the concessions from their interlocutors by speaking to them in the only codes that they understand: the ability to use force in a resolute and overwhelming way if they refuse to come to terms.

No one enters a negotiation willing to compromise something without first being convinced that it does not have a Best Alternative to a Negotiated Agreement (BATNA). And for those following a criminal logic to reach that conclusion, it is first essential to make them feel *credible fear* that *their very existence, not just their fortune and property,* is in danger. Financial and economic sanctions may yield some limited results. Whoever decides to announce in advance that it renounces the use of any form of force in order to bring to reason that peculiar type of counterparts would have lost all negotiating leverage beforehand.

4. **The parallel economy of the new criminal oligarchy feeds off the illegal operations carried out with its global partners: trafficking drugs, weapons and people, and money laundering.** The international sanctions targeting the traditional economy of those countries (oil, sugar, tobacco, tourism) do not affect them to the point of overthrowing those who control power. The clandestine illicit businesses continue to provide them with the essential resources from the underground economy to repress the population.

5. **The Cuban Mafia State is now a colonial power in Venezuela (Cubazuela).** The dictatorial oligarchies in both

countries have merged into a **transnational criminal enterprise**, attracting the collaboration of other anti-Western governments (Russia, Iran, China) as well as some terrorist and drug trafficking organizations (ELN, FARC, Hezbollah). Castro and Maduro also have accomplices in the rulers in Bolivia and Nicaragua (Evo Morales, and Daniel Ortega). The downfall of Morales was a terrible blow to this regional network of production and distribution of drugs.

6. **The head of the regional destabilizing hydra is in Havana.** Changing the regime of governance in Venezuela is indispensable, but insufficient to guarantee long-term regional democratic stability. The Mafia State will continue to make use of its asymmetric, hybrid, total war strategy to replace unfriendly governments with unconditional allies that intend to be eternally in power. While it is obvious that the socio-economic problems of those countries are not fabricated by Havana or Caracas, -as was the case in Ecuador, Chile, and Colombia-, some of the professional agitators that generate the destabilizing violence were previously recruited and trained by Cubazuela. That is not new. It repeats the same pattern of past times when guerrilla groups went to Cuba for training and to practice military actions that were to be later implemented in their countries, professional agitators are now recruited and operational plans to destabilize democratic governments — including the means for their logistical and financial coverage — are also designed in advance and put on hold to be implemented at the right moment. The goal is to build the capability of taking advantage of any local justified grievance and quickly turn it into a destructive generalized chaos that potentially may bring down or wear out unfriendly governments and even their democratic constitutional regimes of governance.

Without a doubt, the challenge pose by Mafia States is immense, but inaction would be a greater risk. Without putting a curb on Cubazuela and its subversive strategy for the region, there will be no security, democracy, or stability in this Hemisphere.

Mafia regimes never respect the human rights of the citizenry nor live at peace with the democracies of the international community.

Venezuela:
A State that became a criminal organization

Maibort Petit

Maibort Petit is a recognized independent investigative re-
porter with over 20 years of experience covering drug
trafficking, international money laundering within and outside the justice systems. Having a very extensive and
impressive educational background which includes under-
graduate and graduate work in Latin American Politics at
the University of La Sorbonne and Paris III, Foreign Policy
at the Foreign Ministry of Venezuela and as a candidate in
the PhD program in Political Science at the Central University of Venezuela.

Her expertise has been recognized worldwide. Her consulting services included communication crisis, conflict
management, Intelligence Analysis relating to major criminal activities and organized criminal groups in Latin
America. She is the author of several books on these
topics.

Maibort Petit has received numerous awards for her investigative reporting, recently by EnTV and for her community
work by the NY Senate. Currently, she is a resident of New
York City working as an independent researcher for several
firms and ONG's in NYC and Washington DC.

The conversion of Venezuela into a criminal enterprise is the result
of the plan that Hugo Chávez Frías conceived from the very moment he attempted to take power by violent means. The *Caracazo*

of February 27th, 1989[88] and the coup attempts on February 4th [89] and November 27th, 1992[90] were only an advance of the macabre plan that he concocted for years, of which that "for the time being"[91] he pronounced hours after his first and failed insubordination, marked one of the first episodes of the thriller-by-installments triggered by such events, already indicating the nature of the government he intended to establish in his country.

Since his raise to the presidency on February 2nd, 1999 as a result of the December 1998 elections, Chávez gradually implemented his plan based on a new political system that would later become a criminal network. This was achieved as he put into practice the changes he had in mind, for whose success destroying the institutions was a must. The Constitution of the Republic emanated from the National Constituent Assembly was the first step, followed by decisions made and actions taken from the Miraflores Palace, with the public powers already subservient to Chavez's will. This started the disruption of the fundamentals of the existing democratic system which, albeit weak and defective, still offered opportunities for participation and space for citizen liberties and the functioning of institutions.[92]

---

[88] "El Caracazo: ¿conspiración de Hugo Chávez?". *El Estímulo*. 27 February 2019. http://elestimulo.com/climax/el-caracazo-conspiracion-de-hugo-Chávez/

[89] "4 de Febrero: Golpe de Estado que marcó la historia en Venezuela". *CZN Mundo*. February 4, 2016. https://mundo.culturizando.com/4-de-febrero-rebelion-militar-que-marco/

[90] "FOTOS y VIDEOS | ¿Recuerdas lo que sucedió el 27 de noviembre de 1992? *El Estímulo*. November 27, 2017. http://elestimulo.com/blog/fotos-y-videos-recuerdas-lo-que-sucedio-el-27-de-noviembre-de-1992/

[91] YouTube. "Hugo Chávez 4 de Febrero 1992". https://www.youtube.com/watch?v=VBUo-pYeVfQ

[92] "¿Cómo fue el proceso constituyente de 1999?; por Carlos García Soto". *Prodavinci*. 20 May 2017. http://historico.prodavinci.com/blogs/como-fue-el-proceso-constituyente-de-1999-por-carlos-garcia-soto/

Behind the scenes, the government of Cuba, with Fidel Castro at its head, moved the strings for Hugo Chávez' actions: as it was learned years later, since 1997 — with the arrival of 29 undercover Cuban agents on Margarita Island — the dictator collaborated with the coup-monger colonel in intelligence, security and computer tasks, and then in his electoral campaign. Such participation was extended to limits still unknown, yet suspected to having gained control of the Venezuelan security apparatus[93]. Nothing happened at random, because every action followed a previously conceived plan, the strategy devised by Chávez and Castro, which consisted in setting up the oppressive regime ruling Venezuela today.

Among the actions taken, one executed in 2005 was a master's play to get rid of the obstacle that the United States represented for achieving the goals set from Havana, in which drug trafficking and the criminal industry had the leading roles. Accusing it of espionage, Chávez expelled the US Drug Enforcement Administration (DEA) from Venezuela.[94]

He also ended cooperation with the East Joint Interagency Task Force, which controlled flights and ships in the Caribbean and on the north coast of South America. The path of the revolution was now unobstructed.

Subsequently the Bolivarian National Armed Force (FANB in Spanish) assumed the anti-drug operations divided by strategic areas. In theory, they would counter drug trafficking, but the facts showed that drug trafficking boomed ever since instead, aided by the government and including a new element, Petróleos de Venezuela S.A. (PDVSA) as a distribution channel for narcotics and an

---

[93] "Las relaciones desmedidas". *El País*. 30 March 2014. Available at:
https://elpais.com/internacional/2014/03/28/actualidad/1396026665_272257.html

[94] "Hugo Chávez suspendió a la DEA en Venezuela". *El Universo*. 9 August 2005. Available at:
https://www.eluniverso.com/2005/08/09/0001/14/F92719B658CC4D2CB68423B3EF0A0268.html

instrument for legitimizing the profits obtained from such criminal activity.[95] [96] Experts have successfully identified 89 individuals and companies operating in at least 26 countries through which the regime diverted USD 28 billion from the State oil company.

The drug trafficking business emerged in Cuba around the 1980s. Exchanging arms for cocaine would be the first approach of the Cuban Communist Party. The drugs confiscated during Cuban enforcement operations, far from being destroyed, would go to foreign smugglers or traffickers. American weapons shipped from Vietnam would be delivered to Colombian insurgents.[97] As a State policy, Castro set out to destroy US society and promoted shipments of drugs by the Colombian cartels. Eventually the traffic thrived and became a source of income for the regime. Under Cuba's guidance, Chávez formed an alliance with the Revolutionary Armed Forces of Colombia (FARC in Spanish) and the National Liberation Army (ELN in Spanish). These Colombian

---

[95] "España y Pdvsa: escenarios del lavado de dinero más grande de Venezuela". *Panam Post*. 20 May 2019.
https://es.panampost.com/sabrina-martin/2019/05/20/espana-y-pdvsa-lava-dode-dinero-venezuela/?cn-reloaded=1

[96] "AN sigue recabando información sobre red de lavado de dinero en Pdvsa". *Tenemos Noticias*. 9 November 2018.
https://tenemosnoticias.com/noticia/contralora-pdvsa-comisinlavado-459664/1035645

[97] Marcelo Fernández-Zayas, "Cuba: Historia del narcotráfico". *Guaracabuya*. Órgano Oficial de la Sociedad Económica de Amigos del País. http://ami-gospais-guaracabuya.org/oagmf007.php

terrorist organizations became the world's leading suppliers of co-caine. [98] [99] [100] The guerrillas were joined by Venezuelan security forces trained by Cuba´s counterintelligence, which helped them to reorganize and eradicate any opposition to Chávez. That was the birth of what was later known as the *Cartel de los Soles* –the name comes from the badges on the epaulets of the Venezuelan generals, known as "suns".[101]

The New Criminal Venezuelan Regime

The Castro-Chavez plan contemplated proclaiming "21st Century Socialism" and extending it throughout the region with the support of ideologically related regimes — Bolivia, Ecuador, Nicaragua, Iran. Many of them joined the Bolivarian Alternative for Latin America and the Caribbean (ALBA in Spanish), a criminal web that underpins the dictatorship. It was endorsed by institutions subjected to its will, and kept it shielded from any attempt to topple it.

Guided by Castro, Chávez established a new economic and political model in Latin America to counter US influence, a goal that was favored by high oil prices. Although his personal charisma and military experience served him well in that pursuit, it

---

[98] 'Las FARC son el cartel de drogas más grande del mundo': expertos". *Vanguardia.*, Colombia. 10 January 2011
https://www.vanguardia.com/deportes/mundial-de-futbol/las-farc-son-el-cartel-dedrogas-mas-grande-del-mundo-expertos-JBVL88128

[99] "Las FARC triplican su cocaína". *El Mundo* 4 March 2015.
https://www.elmundo.es/internacional/2015/03/04/54f622f322601ddc778b4576.html

[100] "Las nuevas guerras que libra Colombia después de las FARC". *El Mundo.* 29 June 2019.
https://www.elmundo.es/internacional/2019/06/29/5d12096dfdddff7c338b45df.html

[101] Christopher Dickey, "How Cuba Helped Make Venezuela a Mafia State". *The Daily Beast.*6 April 2018
https://www.thedailybeast.com/how-cuba-helped-make-venezuela-a-mafia-state

was his willingness to spend millions of dollars from the PDVSA funds what in the end brought it about.

The criminal regime has managed to remain in power despite the sanctions imposed by the US and the support that Juan Guaidó, president of the National Assembly (AN in Spanish) and recognized as interim president by the United States, Canada and more than 50 other countries, has rallied around him after denouncing Nicolás Maduro's usurpation of the Presidency. Maduro reelected himself in a clearly illegitimate and fraudulent balloting exercise. Under his administration the economy contracted by 50 percent; at least 10.5 percent of the Venezuelan population now live as refugees, while the country's instability intensifies, thus imposing huge burdens on its regional neighbors from the ripple effect it triggers. This is what Douglas Farrah defines as the Joint Bolivarian Criminal Company, some kind of consortium of criminal State and non-State actors which, together with the FARC, work in concert for the expansion of their ideological project.[102] The Joint Bolivarian Criminal Company is defined as a unique structure assembled with direct participation of the State, acting criminally and operating through multiple economic fields and police jurisdictions. Such criminal action relies on State entities, illegal dealings and organized crime groups that undermine the rule of law, democratic governance and US alliances in the West.

So, when oil prices fell and brought down revenues, Maduro resorted to other sources of financing, that is, crime and the illegal enterprise, including fake oil sales, drug trafficking, systematic asset purchases, illegal mining, and fake infrastructure projects and bank transfers. The growing number of high-ranking officers, top-

---

[102] The United States. Department of Justice. Office of Public Affairs. "Two Members of Billion-Dollar Venezuelan Money Laundering Scheme Arrested". *Justice News*. 25 July 2018
https://www.justice.gov/opa/pr/two-members-billion-dollar-venezuelan-money-laundering-scheme-arrested

level officials, judges, businessmen and people close to the Venezuelan government involved in drug trafficking and / or money laundering who are being investigated in the US is alarming. These are not improvised statements, they are based on investigations, such as the Report on the International Narcotics Control Strategy (INCSR) that the State Department presents annually to the US Congress. The report established that Venezuela did not comply with the international anti-narcotics treaties and failed to combat drug trafficking and prosecute corrupt or suspected drug trafficking officials, including those convicted in the United States.

In a stark way, the report accounts for the extensive coca crops along the Colombian-Venezuelan border and remarks that some of the chemicals used to produce cocaine are trafficked through Venezuela, although the amount is still unknown. It denounces that the country became a favorite drug trafficking route in the West. In 2018, drug trafficking and its related violence were favored by a weak judicial system, very scarce cooperation for drug control and the permissive and corrupt environment of the Maduro government. It is noted that since 2015 the National Anti-Narcotics Office of Venezuela (ONA in Spanish) has not provided statistics on domestic drug use. It highlights facilities the authorities provided to the FARC and the ELN for drug trafficking. Sanctions imposed by the Treasury Department on 22 individuals and 27 companies with Venezuela connections signaled a poor contribution by the South American country to the fight against international drug trafficking. Most of the illicit drugs that went through Venezuela were intended for the Caribbean, Central America, the US, West Africa and Europe.[103]

---

[103] United States Department of State. Bureau of International Narcotics and Law Enforcement Affairs. *International Narcotics Control. Strategy Report. Drug and Chemical Control. Volume I.* March 2019. https://www.state.gov/wp-content/uploads/2019/04/INCSR-Vol-INCSR-Vol.-I-1.pdf

On the other hand, the State Department said that Venezuela offers plenty of opportunities for financial abuse, which coupled with the lack of political will of the government, limited bilateral cooperation, the unstable economy and endemic corruption, make the country vulnerable to money laundering and financial crimes. Money exchange and price controls offer numerous opportunities for currency manipulation and the arbitration of assets, and force many legitimate merchants to get involved in illegal actions to access the currencies that enable them to operate. **This facilitates money laundering.** Also, Maduro administration officials irregularly channeled hundreds of millions of dollars from PDVSA to US and Europeans banks. Similarly, the report warns that the government maintains a large number of extra budgetary accounts in foreign currencies, lacking transparency and supervision, which makes them vulnerable to corruption.[104]

Significant and indicative of the veracity of these assertions is the fact that the name of Hugo Chávez Frías came out in the trial in which Joaquín Guzmán Loera, aka "El Chapo" was convicted of drug trafficking. There, Alexander Cifuentes, former secretary of the drug lord, explained that since 2008, *"el Loco"* — as Chapo Guzmán called the president — sent them cocaine. He said that El Chapo was looking for a place in the Dominican Republic to land his aircrafts coming from Venezuela and then send the cargo over to Mexico.[105]

---

[104] United States Department of State. Bureau of International Narcotics and Law Enforcement Affairs. *International Narcotics Control. Strategy Report.. Money Laundering. Volume II*. March 2019.
https://www.state.gov/wp-content/uploads/2019/03/INCSR-Vol-INCSR-Vol.-2-pdf.pdf

[105] Mailbort Petit, "El Chapo Guzmán se refería a Hugo Chávez como 'el Loco', salen a relucir los negocios de Venezuela con el cártel de Sinaloa". *El Tiempo Latino*.14 January 2019.
http://eltiempolatino.com/news/2019/jan/14/el-chapo-guzman-se-refria-hugo-chavez-como-el-loco/

In the face of all the evidence and open investigations in the US against the organized crime headed by Maduro, Florida Senator Marco Rubio asked Attorney General William Barr to create a special team to unify all inquiries and file charges against the Venezuelan official.

Senator Rubio argues that Maduro benefits from and supports multiple criminal organizations, which makes him a threat to regional and US security and stability. Hence, gathering evidence and information about the crimes of the Venezuelan president must be coordinated efficiently. Maduro acts with the help of Cuba, Russia, China, Turkey and Iran in fruitful transnational criminal enterprises that will generate money and power to his advantage.[106] Earlier, Rubio had asked US President Donald Trump to designate the Maduro regime and the *"colectivos"* as terrorist organizations.[107] In 2018 several US senators asked the Secretary of State, Mike Pompeo, to designate Venezuela as a "State sponsor of terrorism."

There are efforts, then, to encircle the Venezuelan criminal regime from all possible flanks, and the standard bearer doing this has been the US, which has implemented significant measures — such as channeling PDVSA funds to the interim government of Guaidó. However, it's not enough. **To stop this criminal organization and its allies it is imperative that the Bolivarian criminal web**

---

[106] "Rubio propone investigar a Maduro y sus operaciones de crimen organizado". *El Nuevo Herald* 7 June 2019
https://www.elnuevoherald.com/noticias/mundo/america-latina/venezuela es/article231306923.html

[107] "Rubio pide que régimen de Maduro y colectivos sean designados organizaciones terroristas". Radio Televisión Martí 5 April 2019.
https://www.radiotelevisionmarti.com/a/rubiopide-regimen-maduro-colectivos-sean-designados-organizaciones-terroristas/235713.html

be confronted by a parallel network comprised by the US and its partners.[108]

The Price of Loyalty

Like any company, this one headed by Maduro has a price. And the fact is that, as political science expert Bruce Bueno de Mesquita proposes, the loyalty of the military who support the regime might well dissolve if they were offered a suitable reward. His statement responds to the offer of immunity Guaidó extended to FANB officers in exchange for the withdrawal of their support to the usurper. It´s not enough because "they already have immunity with Maduro, plus a flow of wealth that has been guaranteed so far." The offer will only be attractive if the officers can be persuaded that the regime is collapsing and that they have no choice but to retire and are allowed to continue enjoying their fortunes in freedom under the incoming governments.[109]

But it is vital that the US and its partners contribute funds so that Guaidó can persuade the top brass to turn coats for him rather than remaining loyal to the money they get from Maduro. A mass defection of senior officers would change the political landscape dramatically, since power in Venezuela is held by the higher echelons of the military. And it is not that the ruler lacks credit, but his merit lies in "knowing how to access the money and who must be paid among the top brass and who must be paid among the top-

---

[108] Douglas Farraw, Caitlyn Yates. "La Última Resistencia de Maduro: La supervivencia de Venezuela mediante la empresa criminal conjunta bolivariana". IBI Consultants, LLC y National Defense University (INSS) April 2019. https://www.ibiconsultants.net/_pdf/maduros-last-stand-spanish10640.pdf

[109] Antonio Maria Delgado, "Experto: el futuro de Venezuela depende de un puñado de chavistas... y pueden ser comprados". El Nuevo Herald. 6 February 2019. https://www.elnuevoherald.com/noticias/mundo/america-latina/venezuela-es/article225621770.html

level civil servants (…) [for Maduro] like all dictators, depends on the inner circle that surrounds him."[110]

Cuba as Mentor

"Havana collaborated with Venezuela in the creation of a criminal-terrorist conduit designed to channel funds and drugs from Latin America to the Middle East, in exchange for providing safe haven to foreign fighters and Islamic terrorists," says Joseph Humire, executive director of the Center for a Secure Free Society (SFS).

In 2003, Chávez asked the Cuban vice president, Ramiro Valdés, for advice on immigration. With the help of the Cuban University of Computer Science, the G2 installed the new Venezuelan immigration system. During 2009-12, the system, under Cuban control, "delivered passports, visas and identity documents to at least 173 Middle Eastern Islamic militants, many of them suspected of maintaining ties with the Lebanese terrorist organization Hezbollah (...)." This establishes that "Cuba has played a primary role in guaranteeing terrorists a robust presence in the Western hemisphere, even facilitating their entry into North America".[111] Passports were also provided to members of ancient dynasties in the Middle East. This is more than just moving terrorists, and reveals a "dark clandestine web" between Venezuela and Syria whose goal is unknown, but in which a warlike purpose is envisioned.

In the Venezuelan case, the term "narco State" has become obsolete, the pertinent definition being, due to the country's links and

---

[110] "Experto en dictaduras habla sobre Venezuela". *VOA*. 31 May 2019. https://www.voanoticias.com/a/bueno-de-mesquita-entrevista-con-voa/4940466.html

[111] Joseph Humire "Obama comete un error al eliminar a Cuba de lista negra del terrorismo". *Panam Post* 16 April 2015. https://es.panampost.com/joseph-humire/2015/04/16/obama-comete-un-error-al-eliminar-acuba-de-lista-negra-del-terrorismo/

activities with drug traffickers, a "parallel State", where Tareck El Aissami plays the leading role. It is "a civil-paramilitary criminal structure resembling a State, growing within the State and having more power than the actual State. "According to this, the country is divided into separate territories where drug traffickers, money launderers and irregular forces, such as terrorists and militias, operate. "Venezuela is a parallel State being occupied and controlled by extra regional actors that also control Cuba".[112]

From the above-mentioned reasons, it can be ascertained that Maduro is negotiable, but other characters like El Aissami are not. More than stopping the regime, the main goal must be to bring to a halt the Bolivarian revolution, which seeks to change the geopolitical map of Latin America. It has been disclosed that there is "a channel for crime and terrorism, managed by Venezuela, which sends drugs and funds to the Middle East and brings back foreign fighters or Islamic terrorists to the Western Hemisphere." Venezuela would play an important role in the proliferation of weapons of mass destruction in Iran, by providing that country's controversial nuclear program access to nuclear technology in Argentina. And although these are yet to be confirmed, there are reports suggesting that the Venezuelan government "has provided and acquired strategic minerals, metals and materials for Iran's weapons of mass destruction programs".[113]

So much interest in Venezuela is due to the desire that it becomes a logistics base, a channel of access to the West for these Middle East nations and Hezbollah. "Iran would not allow a way out in

---

[112] Carolina Morales-Chataing, "Los negocios sucios de Tareck El Alssaimi y su familia con Hezbolá (parte 3)". Radio Televisión Martí 19 May 2019. https://www.radiotelevisionmarti.com/a/no-esta-isto-losnegocios-sucios-de-tareck-el-alssaimi-y-su-familia-con-hezbol%C3%A1-(parte-3)/239176.html

[113] Joseph Humire "Venezuela se ha ganado sus galones como amenaza a seguridad de EE.UU.". *Panam Post*. 6 April 2015 https://es.panampost.com/joseph-humire/2015/03/26/venezuela-se-ha-ganado-sus-galones-como-amenaza-a-seguridad-de-ee-uu/.

Venezuela, as much as they would not allow a solution in Syria, unless Iran negotiates such solution." Their goal would be for Venezuela to become the Syria of Latin America. An indication of this is that the same actors that caused the conflict in the Middle Eastern nation also generated it in the South American one: Russia and Iran, manipulating economic and humanitarian circumstances to boost what they call "people's anarchy" and others call civil war. This would be carried out by way of the Venezuelan Corporation of Military Industries (CAVIM in Spanish). In 2004, the president of Iran and Chávez broke an alliance between their armed forces that was in fact "a logistical alliance to send and receive what is prohibited to Iran by the international community because of its missile and nuclear programs."

Considered as expendable, Maduro's government would be just *ad interim*, because the real intention of the promoters of the conflict is to uplift Tareck El Aissami to the presidency. Maintaining the massive displacement of Venezuelans is another fundamental objective, aimed to infiltrate Hezbollah members throughout Latin America and even the United States. "Iran, Cuba and the FARC in Colombia will be in charge (…) [since] that of Venezuela is a conflict of extra regional actors that threatens the region. It is a conflict designed to be exported". Therefore, there cannot be a solution for Venezuela as long as Cuba, Iran, Syria, Russia and China remain in the country.[114]

---

[114] María Angélica Correa. "En Venezuela no hay salida si no salen Cuba, Irán, Siria, Rusia y China de ese país". *Perú 21*. 14 November 2017. https://peru21.pe/mundo/venezuela-hay-salida-salen-cuba-iran-siria-rusia-china-ese-pais-384214-noticia/

Making up of the Venezuelan Criminal Industry

The breeding ground of this criminal industry in Venezuela has been corruption and a weak rule of law, as confirmed by the Organized Crime Research Center (Insigth Crime),[115] which established that this factors helped make the country a key hub for drug trafficking from Colombia to the US and Europe, with the security forces assuming a leading role through the *"Cartel de los Soles"* in the early decades of the 21st century. Similarly, corrupt members of the FANB became providers of armament for the black market, mainly favoring the FARC and the ELN. These two, along with the vernacular guerrillas — the Bolivarian Liberation Forces or Patriotic Forces for National Liberation (FBL-FPLN in Spanish) — operate from Venezuelan territory, committing themselves to human trafficking, money laundering and trafficking chemicals for the illegal drug industry. The lengthy Venezuelan-Colombian border, the former's extensive coastline on the Caribbean, its jungles and sparsely populated savannas and its proximity to Puerto Rico, Trinidad & Tobago and the Dominican Republic, make of Venezuela an important drug trafficking route.

Drug trafficking used to operate in Venezuela by way of foreign mafias. From the 1980's and throughout the 90's, the country was a transit place for cocaine and heroin from Colombia to Europe, via connections with the Cali Cartel. But the Venezuelan crisis had a negative effect, the Colombian drug traffickers gained ground and then the FANB got involved, at first as facilitators of the neighboring country's narcos, a role from which they evolved to take the leadership during the Chávez administration. The DEA was no longer a hindrance and, in the face of Colombia's resolute fight

---

[115] "Venezuela Profile". Insigth Crime.10 November 2017.
https://www.insightcrime.org/venezuela-organized-crime-news/venezuela/

against the guerrillas under Plan Colombia, the FARC and ELN sought refuge in Apure, Zulia and Táchira, where they now move freely thanks to the alleged Venezuelan Government financing and protection. Chávez' statement that the FARC "is not the enemy" of Venezuela was revealing, and his refusal to classify the group as a terrorist one exposed his sympathy toward the guerrilla's ideology. The number of reports about FANB weapons and ammunition in the hands of the guerrillas grew up and they became obvious when Colombia found data linking Chávez with the insurgents in the computer of "Raúl Reyes."

In the early 21st century the links of the Government with organized crime deepened, as elements of the National Guard and the Army went from accepting bribes for allowing the passage of the drug, to storing and transporting the cargoes themselves. Now the military and their political allies were not intermediaries anymore, they directly managed the deal. The outlook did not change with the ascent of Maduro to power: his promise to combat crime was only lip service: corruption and politicization of the system were exacerbated instead, giving almost an institutional character to criminality The FARC's public support of Maduro was revealing enough.[116]

The criminality that these groups represent is compounded by the so-called *colectivos*, the militia, and the armed gangs that act with absolute impunity throughout the country. Such state of insecurity imposed an informal curfew at dusk, as people rushed to their homes for protection. The Sinaloa Cartel establishing cells in Venezuela is something that has not yet been ruled out.

---

[116] "Las FARC manifiestan su apoyo a Maduro". *El Nacional.* 22 April 2017. http://www.elnacional.com/noticias/latinoamerica/las-farc-manifiestan-apoyo-maduro_178554

Cartel of the Suns

On August 18, 2015, a former member of the Military House and former security chief of Hugo Chávez and Diosdado Cabello, corvette captain Leamsy Salazar, defected and fled the country. Once in the US he denounced crimes, especially drug trafficking, as masterminded by the Venezuelan military top brass and government hierarchs. His depositions as a protected witness of the Southern New York District's Attorney were explosive. He stated that Cabello — former president of the AN and current president of the National Constituent Assembly — is the leader of the Cartel of the Suns. He said he witnessed "situations and conversations that incriminate" Cabello, as well as operations directed by the senior official," and "contributed evidence about places where mountains of dollars in cash from such illicit business are stored, according to sources close to the investigation", which is carried out by the DEA. He also implicated Tareck El Aissami, and José David Cabello, superintendent of Seniat, who he said to be in charge of the cartel's finances. He ratified that PDVSA is used to launder drugs money and accused Chavez's son and the son of former Cuban ambassador to Caracas, Germán Sánchez Otero, as drug traffickers.[117]

Insight Crime documented the crimes of senior officers, active or retired, involved in cocaine trafficking that "for legal reasons" it does not publish completely and only offers "some data of those against whom we believe we have very strong evidence." Thus, they cite, first and foremost, Diosdado Cabello, about whom sources in the US Department of Justice would have revealed on condition of anonymity that "this guy is stuck to his neck in all

---

[117] "El jefe de seguridad del número dos chavista deserta a EE.UU. y le acusa de narcotráfico". *ABC* 18 August 2015.
https://www.abc.es/internacional/20150127/abcivenezuela-cabello-eeuu-201501262129.html

kinds of illegal activities in Venezuela and we are putting together a case against him. But he knows how to protect himself and keep the dirty work at arm's length."

In May 2015, *The Wall Street Journal* revealed that US prosecutors investigated Cabello for drug trafficking and as head of the Cartel of the Suns[118]. The *Journal* mentioned evidence that Leamsy Salazar delivered about his alleged role in the passage of narcotics through Venezuela. Cabello sued the newspaper for defamation, but a court rejected the lawsuit.

Then there is Tareck El Aissami, signaled for allegedly participating in drug trafficking and linked to organized crime in the Caribbean.

We also find Major General Nestor Reverol, Minister of Internal Relations and former commander of the Bolivarian National Guard (GNB in Spanish), charged with drug trafficking in the US[119] who, according to the charges, "alerted drug traffickers of operations against them, obstructed investigations, released arrested drug traffickers and made sure that narcotics seized from traffickers were returned to them." Also, Edylberto Molina Molina, second in command when Venezuela's National Anti-Drug Office (ONA in Spanish) was under Reverol's control. He is accused of being a drug trafficking operator and taking advantage of his position to facilitate the activities of the cartels in Venezuelan territory.

Venezuela's first lady, Cilia Flores, is involved in drug trafficking by association. The case of her nephews — Efraín Antonio Campo

---

[118] "Venezuelan Officials Suspected of Turning Country into Global Cocaine Hub". *The Wall Street Journal*. 18 May 2018.
https://www.wsj.com/articles/venezuelan-officialssuspected-of-turning-country-into-global-cocaine-hub-1431977784

[119] "Néstor Reverol acusado por EEUU de recibir dinero del narcotráfico". *El Impulso*. 1 August 2016
https://www.elimpulso.com/2016/08/01/nestor-reverol-acusado-eeuu-recibir-dinerodel-narcotrafico/

Flores and Francisco Flores de Freitas — convicted of cocaine traf-ficking in the US, [120] is one example; another one another is that of her son, Walter Jacob Gavidia, also investigated.[121] In the first case, the statements by Campo Flores stand out. He said that part of the proceeds from the drug trafficking operation he planned, he would invest in his aunt's re-election campaign.

The links of the Cartel of the Suns with the FARC "were decisive in the development of drug trafficking in Venezuela," because a large number of members of the Colombian group are in Venezue-lan territory participating in the business along with members of the cartel. The approval in 2005 of the Organic Law against Illicit Trafficking and Substance Consumption expanded anti-narcotics operations to all branches of the FANB, with the Cartel of the Suns growing as a result.

Walid Makled, a drug dealer wanted in the United States and who is allegedly in custody of the Venezuelan authorities, was the one who first detailed the activity of the Cartel of the Suns. He main-tained good relations with members of the army and his criminal enterprise gained importance within the Chávez government. His main connections would have been former GNB general and for-mer governor of Carabobo Luis Felipe Acosta Carles, and General Alexis Maniero, former chief of the 7th Regional Army Command in the state of Sucre, who endowed Makled with official creden-tials. He would also maintain links with senior officials of the CICPC and the militia. Makled said that he paid USD 50,000 weekly to Hugo Carvajal, former director of intelligence, and

---

[120] Mailbort Petit, "LO ULTIMO: Juez condena a Narcosobrinos de Cilia Flores y Nicolás Maduro a 18 años de prisión". *Venezuela Política*. 14 December 2017. https://www.maibortpetit.info/2017/12/lo-ultimo-juez-condena-narcosobrinos-de.html

[121] "Hijo de Cilia Flores investigado por sospecha de narcotráfico". *Notilogía* November 2015 https://www.notilogia.com/2015/11/hijo-de-cilia-flores-investigado-por-sospe-cha-de-narcotrafico.html

among his collaborators were GNB general Dalal Burgos and ex captain Ramón Rodríguez Chacín, former minister of the Interior and of Justice. "The Cartel of the Suns is today a disparate network of traffickers, which includes State and non-State actors, but operates with total consent and protection of important figures within the Venezuelan government. Without such crucial political facade, and payments to the right people, smuggling operations would stop".[122]

Investigations by federal agencies in the United States indicate that until mid-2018 at least twenty active Venezuelan generals in high positions, four former ministers, six judges, a large number of public administration officials and five wealthy businessmen would be at the service of drug trafficking. Investigations exposed before Florida, New York and Washington DC courts sustain that there are members of the Venezuelan armed forces and the police who operate in drug trafficking activities.

Evidence on the ties between Venezuelan civil servants, the military and the cartels is abundant and it exposes the structure built up throughout the so-called Bolivarian Revolution, not only to keep in power the current dominant coalition but also to make it impervious to any attempt to overthrow it. An investigation published by *Diario Las Américas* sustains that Hugo Chávez pressed the drug traffickers to get the opposition involved in their trade, in exchange for not being extradited to the United States. For a while the agreements were honored, but then the allies of the *capos* handed them over, first to Venezuelan justice and then allowing their extradition to the US, where they began to report on the structure of drug trafficking in Venezuela.[123]

---

[122] Venezuelan Investigative Unit, "Drug Trafficking Within the Venezuelan Regime: The 'Cartel of the Suns' *Insight Crime*. 17 May 2018 https://www.insightcrime.org/investigations/drug-trafficking-venezuelan-regime-cartel-of-the-sun/

[123] Frank López Ballesteros, "El imperio del narcotráfico estuvo al servicio de Hugo Chávez" *Diario Las Américas*. 8 June 2018.

Tareck El Aissami as kingpin
of the organization

A separate chapter in this plot duly belongs to Tareck El Aissami, former governor of Aragua, former vice president and current Minister of the People's Power for Industries and National Production. The US Treasury Department accused him of drug trafficking in February 2017, and as a result his visa was canceled, his properties in the US were confiscated and he is vetoed to perform financial or commercial transactions with US institutions.

This senior official of the ruling party is accused of allegedly allowing members of the Hezbollah terrorist group to enter Venezuela and assisting them with the aim of expanding espionage and drug trafficking in the region, according to investigations conducted by Venezuela's intelligence service, and quoted by *The New York Times* in May 2019.[124] About this, Makled assured that the official was assisted by his brother, a claim corroborated by Hugo Carvajal in February 2019, when he accused El Aissami of maintaining links with the Shiite Lebanon-based militant organization since 2009. In 2015, the media reopened the issue, this time holding Tareck El Aissami as directly responsible.

Aissami's political militancy began when he was a student at the University of Los Andes (ULA), from which he graduated as a lawyer and where he later on met Adam Chávez, Hugo Chávez's brother, while working as a professor. Then he joined the V Republic Movement and became a member of its board. He headed the so-called *Misión Identidad* during Hugo Cabezas — a fellow

---

https://www.diariolasamericas.com/america-latina/el-imperio-del-narcotrafi-coestuvo-al-servicio-hugo-Chávez-n4152829

[124]Nicholas Casey, "Secret Venezuela Files Warn About Maduro Confidant". *The New York Times*. 2 May 2019.
https://www.nytimes.com/2019/05/02/world/americas/venezuela-maduro-hez-bollah-drugs.html

student at ULA — time as director of the old National Office for Identification and Immigration. In 2005 he was elected to the AN, and in 2007 he went on to occupy the Vice Ministry for Prevention and Citizen Security. After Ramón Rodríguez Chacín resigned from the Ministry of Interior and Justice in 2008, he assumed the ministerial office until October 2012, when he ran for and won the governorship of Aragua. The reform of the penitentiary system under his watch at the Ministry of Interior allowed the emergence of the *"pran"*, a negative leader who controls prisons and directs criminal operations even from inside the detention center.

In 2017, when he was Executive Vice President, the US Treasury Department accused him of drug trafficking and imposed the above mentioned sanctions against him. The US government singled him out again on March 8th, 2019, for evading these sanctions along with his alleged front man, Samark López. It was reported that both men defied the sanctions traveling from Russia to Venezuela aboard private planes provided by US-registered companies. They were charged before a federal court in Manhattan for violations to the Law on Foreign Drug Traffickers with Special Designation.[125] While El Aissami was the governor of Aragua, some mega-gangs emerged in the state that participated in kidnapping, extortion, vehicle theft, drug microtrafficking and other crimes." El Aissami would have facilitated the shipment of narcotics from Venezuela to Mexico and the US thanks to his control of planes that departed from a Venezuelan base, as well as facilitating routes through the country's ports.[126]

---

[125] Venezuela Investigative Unit "US Piles on the Pressure Against Venezuela's El Aissami". *Insight Crime*. 14 March 2019.
https://es.insightcrime.org/noticias/analisis/eeuu-el-aissami-venezuela/

[126] "Tareck El Aissami". *Insight Crime*. 17 June 2019
https://www.insightcrime.org/venezuela-organized-crime-news/tareck-el-aissami/

The Government Expands its Forces

The Venezuelan regime's armor is not limited to state security forces, it also expanded its shield to include the irregular armies known as *"colectivos"*. The whole world saw the *"colectivos"* in action on February 23, 2019, when, together with FAES and GNB troopers, they shot and repressed unarmed civilians trying to enter humanitarian aid to Venezuela through the borders of Colombia and Brazil. At least four people were killed and 285 were injured, including some Pemón aborigins, who decided to take refuge in Brazil. These groups are made up by illegally armed civilians from the Chávez times, self-appointed as assault forces for the defense of the Bolivarian revolution, which gives them impunity to perpetrate offenses like extortion, killing for hire, kidnapping and drug trafficking.

The *colectivos* expressed support for Maduro. A member of one of this groups called Revolutionary Secretariat of Venezuela warned Insight Crime that "if something happens, we will have to go out to defend the Government, because the newcomers will come after us." The government shields itself on several flanks, using either regular and institutional forces indoctrinated to protect the interests, not of the Venezuelan nation, but of the so-called revolution; or organizations born around it, such as the aforementioned Cartel of the Suns, military men who, like the rest, support the government but, above all, the organized crime-based business. On the other hand they count on the Special Actions Force (FAES in Spanish) of the Bolivarian National Police that has become a real death squad. According to the Human Rights NGO Provea, FAES members have been involved in more than 675 extrajudicial executions, mainly in poor districts. They are a police force loyal to Maduro, indoctrinated, violent and ready to kill. Members of the *colectivos* have joined FAES, as confirmed by officials of the PNB and the regular police.

The loyalty that the government exacts from its security forces, who remain silent vis-à-vis the repression and the abuses, is nothing but fear of being victims of persecution, imprisonment and torture, as is the case with many adversaries of the regime.[127]

In short, Venezuela is a dismantled state, turned into a criminal organization. The complexities of the organization, its international alliances and the ability of its members to achieve its goals, have so far enabled it to overcome historical crises and stay in power. At least for the time being.

---

[127] Insight Crime. "Las 2 caras de los 'ejércitos' criminales del régimen de Venezuela". 28 February 2019. https://es.insightcrime.org/noticias/analisis/las-2-caras-de-los-ejercitoscriminales-del-regimen-de-venezuela/

Conclusions

Hugo Achá

When we perform this analysis, it is essential to reach conclusions, which are not simple and are susceptible to debate and refinement; they are not pleasant and will probably bother more than one reader.

As this work shows, one of the necessary conclusions is posed as a question: **Can we design new tools that are agile and flexible enough to face this phenomenon, while maintaining the essence of our democracy?**

The biggest limitations lie in the fact that the West has not yet understood the full nature of this new model, and what is even more serious: for ideological / philosophical reasons, in several countries they refuse to accept its existence.

In fact, even the United States refuses to understand that our adversaries are not interested in following the normal rules, and that those adversaries are as adaptable or more than we are, (and sometimes more intelligent), that they have been able to develop highly efficient and effective strategies, as well as concepts that overcome our preventive measures, evade our controls and elude our capability to react.

This causes governments like the United States to limit the scope of their responses, for example to exclusively law enforcement and the courts, which grants our opponents time, and ample space for reaction, adaptation and maneuver.

It is also necessary to understand and confront the phenomenon to neutralize it. There is an even deeper reason for this: due to the basis and foundation of Western society and the checks and balances inherent in a democracy, the West will never be able to adopt this method of warfare, and remain democracies.

This new way of waging war, which violates every principle of law, engages the underworld without moral restrictions and violates the most fundamental human rights without fear of any consequences, has no way of being adapted, imitated or used by the world democracies.

However, it can be defeated as long as it is understood that we face a different, innovative and bold war model, but which even in all its potential has fewer resources than countries like the United States.

It is necessary to rethink the operational and doctrinal models so that the institutional response of the West may be accompanied by all its military capabilities; that is, to face this total and endless war with the totality of the State capabilities.

Limiting this analysis for reasons of political correctness or cultural preconceptions is to invite defeat.

The responses and strategies to take on this model must be covered with credible, palpable and definite consequences: in such a way that our adversaries can perceive a *credible* threat that *their very existence, not just their fortune and property, is in danger.*

Annexes

Castrochavismo
Organized Crime in the Américas

Carlos Sánchez Berzain

Carlos Sanchez Berzaín is a Constitutionalist Lawyer. He has a master's in political science and another master's in psychology. Sanchez is a university professor, and a founding member of the Ateneo Jurídico Bolivariano.

Carlos Sanchez was on five occasions a State minister and a Member of Parliament in Bolivia. He is specialized in Latin American affairs and is the Executive Director of the Institute for Inter American Democracy. He is exiled in the United States.

www.carlossanchezberzain.com

The author has a long list of publications devoted to the emergence of the new criminal States in Latin America. This is the presentation speech Mr. Sanchez made to his latest book: *Castrochavismo Organized Crime in the Américas*.[128] Sánchez believes this is the name that best describes the transnational organized crime system that usurps political power in Cuba, Venezuela, Bolivia and Nicaragua, which should be treated as an organized crime structure and not as a political process. The gravity, recurrence, and impunity of the crimes committed by Castro-Díaz-Canel, Maduro, Morales, Ortega-Murillo and the members of their regimes, added to the transnational structure they have developed, has reduced the oppressed peoples to a "defenseless condition" and represents the most serious threat to peace and security in the Americas.

The dictatorships that exist today in Cuba, Venezuela, Bolivia and Nicaragua, based on the partnership between Hugo

---

[128] Sánchez Berzain, Carlos. *Castrochavismo Organized Crime in the Américas.* (Miami: Interamerican Institute for Democracy, 2019)

131

Chavez and Fidel Castro, are indeed a structure of "transnational organized crime", not a political process. This points to a fundamental legal, social, and security issue. It is about the continuation of a battle for the truth, starting by calling things by their name, in order to recognize and understand reality objectively and with realism.

In the 21st century, the international community, governments, the academia, the free press and societies have been reluctant — some still are — to recognize that dictatorships have multiplied in the Americas: twenty years later, instead of one — that of Cuba that existed alone in 1999 — there are four dictatorships permanently threatening and conspiring against the region's democracies.

One of my first books in this field is *21ˢᵗ. Century Dictatorship in Bolivia*,[129] which demonstrates with documents that a dictatorship was installed in Bolivia as of 2006. This book retakes and develops the concept of dictatorships that reach power through elections and then go on to liquidate democracy through successive coups. It was first broached by Oswaldo Hurtado, former President of Ecuador, who wrote *Las Dictaduras del siglo XXI: caso Ecuador* (2012).

In my book *Dictatorship and Democracy in the Americas*,[130] I set out to reflect on and demonstrate the existence of two Americas. Not two Americas from a cultural point of view —Latin versus Anglo-Saxon—, not two Americas either from the economic point of view — first world versus third world —, nor two Americas differentiated by their degree of development — developed versus underdeveloped or developing —, not even two Americas defined from a social point of view, but two Americas organized and divided by their essential elements and democratic conditions. A group of dictatorships led by Cuba and made up by Venezuela,

---

[129] Sánchez Berzain, Carlos. *XXI Century Dictatorship in Bolivia*. (Miami: Interamerican Institute for Democracy, 2013)

[130] Sánchez Berzain, Carlos. *Dictatorship and Democracy in the Americas*. (Miami: Interamerican Institute for Democracy, 2017)

Nicaragua, Bolivia, and Rafael Correa's Ecuador, that managed to aligned with them the Kirchners' Argentina, the Brazil of the Workers Party and Lula/Rousseff, while projecting a widespread presence and control in Central America (through PetroCaribe), and the Organization of American States (OAS).

These two Americas result in a confrontational axis in which, on one end, the perpetual and arbitrary control of power, using ideology as a pretext, trademark the dictatorships; while on the other, democracies feature respect for human rights, alternation in power, accountability and free elections, attributes specifically protected by the inter-American system, and enshrined — among others — in the Inter-American Democratic Charter.

Now I introduce "Castrochavismo", a neologism, a single word. A word that represents two characters that marked the history of the early 21st century in the Americas: Castro and Chávez. This first word of the title is followed by a phrase that, in addition to pointing out the fundamental characteristic of those above named, is a definition. "Organized Crime in the Americas" describes the system of institutionalized, recurrent, transnational and unpunished crime, as a form of power management and usurpation in States under dictatorial control, which right now are Cuba (with Raúl Castro-Díaz-Canel), Venezuela (with Nicolás Maduro), Bolivia (with Evo Morales) and Nicaragua (with Daniel Ortega-Rosario Murillo).

This is a story that you are well aware of, but I will retell it anyway. In 1999 there was only one dictatorship in the Americas: Castro's Cuba. After more than 40 years in power, he was enduring the worst of what he called a "Special Period". His project was dying: the new decade had seen the Berlin Wall fall, and the Soviet Union crumble; as a consequence, his own dictatorship, as the parasitic entity that it always was, had been left without a sponsor and its economic support. Then Lt. Colonel Hugo Chávez happened to win the presidential elections and take over the Venezuelan government. A coup monger flattered and protected by Fidel Castro, he immediately ran to Cuba where they formed or reactivated an alliance, a criminal society, which at the beginning was indistinguishable, but eventually changed and branded the history of the 21st century in the Americas. Thus, what today we call *Castrochavismo* was created.

From 1959 to 1999, the Cuban dictatorship was known as "Castroism." From 1999 onwards, it is "Castrochavismo," led by Hugo Chavez until his death. Ever since the alliance with Chávez, the new project recognized his clear leadership due to the contribution and control of Venezuela's money and oil, which he used as the main instruments for maneuvering, coercion, destabilization and bribery. It began as progressive leftist populism, and was successively called the ALBA Movement (Bolivarian Alliance for the Peoples of Our America, in Spanish); Bolivarian Movement; after a few years Socialism of the 21st Century, and nowadays Castrochavismo. Since its inception, **Castrochavismo sought to present itself as a political, populist and democratic movement but, as the facts and the objective reality indicate, such characteristics were only a disguise, an alibi or a mask to hide the true nature of the largest conglomerate of transnational organized crime to ever hold political power.**

When in 1999 Chávez and Castro joined forces, a very fragile Chávez, with an unstable government, sought stability and political support. These he got from Castro's dictatorial security system and his repression services, which would end up being imposed on Venezuela. Fidel Castro received money and oil to get Cuba out of famine, and resumed his failed and dying project, that he calls "Revolution". With this he had controlled Cuba since 1959; had covered the Americas with blood supporting the guerrillas of the 60s; continued to shed blood in the 70s and 80s with urban guerrillas, sabotage, narco guerrillas and terrorism. He even went beyond the Americas to Angola, but that intervention became inoperable because the Soviet source of financing collapsed, thus bringing the Cold War to its end.

Yet Castro would receive a new source of financing for his conspiratorial and criminal actions when Chávez surrendered to him not only Venezuela's money and oil but, as we clearly see today, the entire country. This allowed the only Latin American dictator at the time to reactivate genuine Castroism under the mantle of the Bolivarian movement or ALBA project, and disguise it as democracy. With Venezuela's money, he started conspiracies, which led to the fall and overthrow of democratic leaders. The first one occurs in Argentina, with the fall of President De La Rúa; then it happens in Ecuador and it is Jamil Mahuad who pays the price; the third one is the overthrow of President Gonzalo Sánchez de Lozada in Bolivia; the fourth takes place in Ecuador, with the fall of President Lucio Gutiérrez. They also overthrew the OAS Secretary General, Miguel Ángel Rodríguez, who had just been elected. A false case of corruption was planted in Costa Rica, where Rodríguez ended up being illegally detained, making room for José Miguel Insulza to arrive at the OAS. The rest is known history: Chavez's dominance and leadership over Latin America until his death, inherited by the Castro dictators in Cuba.

At the onset of the new century, Chávez and Castro started a path intent on destroying democracy in the Americas, which was promptly aggravated by the terrorist attacks of September 11, 2001 against the United States. As a result, the region got politically abandoned by the leader of the free world. The nascent Castrochavista organization grew up with Lula da Silva taking power with the Workers' Party in Brazil. Lula used his mandates, to strengthen the project's extraordinary flow of economic resources resorting to transnational corruption. A sample of such crimes, among others, is the infamous case "Lava Jato-Odebrecht."

The destruction of democracy becomes self-evident: the exiles, who had been purely Cuban, became regional as Venezuelans, Bolivians, Nicaraguans, Ecuadorians, Argentineans, and Central Americans flee their countries. Former Ecuadorean President Oswaldo Hurtado points out the issue in view of Rafael Correa's overrun of the institutions and the Republic. I denounced the existence and consolidation of the dictatorship of Morales in Bolivia. Carlos Alberto Montaner, from his columns and programs, notes the expansion of the Castro power. Armando Valladares, in his lectures and denunciations calls them out, and many other authors testify to the proliferation of dictatorial regimes promoted by Chávez and Castro. These works, lectures and forums attract attention, but the reaction is of disbelief, with the argument that the dictatorships articulated by Chavez and Castro continued to be democracies because they held elections. Elections in Venezuela, elections in Nicaragua, elections in Ecuador and Bolivia, while bypassing and hiding that they had destroyed all the legal and constitutional order, annihilated the rule of law and created a new reality with infamous laws[131] that violate human rights and eliminate the fundamental guarantees, so that they could establish a quasi-legal regime that is criminal in nature.

It is important to remember that the Inter-American Democratic Charter, signed in Lima on September 11th, 2001 by all the countries in the Americas, with the exception of the Cuban dictatorship, has mandatory value for the member States of the OAS. It is a mandatory instrument deliberately ignored throughout the period of control of the OAS by Castrochavismo under Secretary General Insulza, and partially applied in the most recent tenure.

The Inter-American Democratic Charter establishes in its Article Number 1 that "The peoples of the Americas have the right to democracy and their governments have the obligation to promote and defend it." Article Number 3 mandates that "Essential elements of

---

[131] "Infamous Law is a norm that, elaborated and established following the formal procedure for its creation, violates in its object or contents the human rights or fundamental freedoms." They are laws that the Castrochavista regimes approve with the control they have of the Legislative Power, uphold with their command of constitutionality control, and apply with the control they have of the prosecutors and judges of the regime. In "Political Prisoners of Organized Crime Regimes," Carlos Sánchez Berzain. Infobae. May 28, 2018

representative democracy include, *inter alia*, respect for human rights and fundamental freedoms, access to and exercise of power in accordance with the rule of law, the holding of periodic, free, and fair elections based on secret balloting and universal suffrage as an expression of the sovereignty of the people, the pluralistic system of political parties and organizations, and the separation of powers and independence of the branches of government."

Since 2003, I repeatedly maintained in my writings, conferences, press statements, academic papers and books, that the absence of just one of these "essential" elements makes democracy disappear, and that in those countries with governments established by Castro and Chávez, as in Venezuela, Ecuador under Correa, Bolivia with Morales, and Nicaragua with Ortega, none of the essential elements of democracy are met or exist, with the aggravating element that they all have political prisoners and exiles, legalized persecution and have liquidated freedom of the press.

Today's elections are used as a means of simulation, even in Cuba, where they just falsified the reform of a constitution that is a mere statute of control for the dictatorship. The manipulation of balloting processes with the existence of none of the essential elements of democracy by Castrochavismo highlights another chain of crimes that leads us to a concept that I propose to be studied by political science, that of "electoral dictatorship".

An electoral dictatorship is a "political regime that by force or violence concentrates all power in a person or in a group or organization that represses human rights and fundamental freedoms and uses illegitimate elections, neither free nor fair, with fraud and corruption, to perpetuate itself indefinitely in power". It is an expression of a chain of crimes that highjacks the popular will and the sovereignty of the peoples. In an electoral dictatorship "you vote, but you don't elect." Watch out, "you vote, but you don't elect", in order to simulate democracy and claim international legitimacy, with well lubricated propaganda and manipulation mechanisms by some international organizations. It has worked for them albeit with increasing difficulties because the crimes are already evident, and the citizens resist and revolt.

In its history, Castrochavismo went through an initial stage in which it called itself Socialism of the 21st Century, an ideological cover to pose as a progressive and democratic project. It tried unsuccessfully to survive operating within the Sao Paulo Forum, an instrument born as a leftist coalition organized by Cuba in response to the collapse of the Soviet Union. It also creates bodies and organizations claiming to be populist, or leftist, claiming to be progressive, socialist, and some even communist, always trying to stay in the field of politics, when actually what this is all about is covering up a criminal structure.

During these 20 years of Castrochavismo, a very interesting phenomenon occurred on the mutation from pure Castroism to Castrochavismo. The leader, the boss, was the one who put the money and that was unquestionably Hugo Chávez, but it turns out that Chávez dies — a most convenient event for the Cuban dictatorship — and the Castros and Cuba assume the leadership. Such relay of command lifts them up to the leadership of Latin America, first at the OAS Summit in Panama where there is an encounter with the president of the United States, and an opening that recognizes such leadership by the oldest dictatorship in Latin America. If Chavez had still been alive, surely the term would be Chávez-castrismo, but today the criminal group is under the clear and undisputable leadership of Raúl Castro and Cuba.

Excluded from the OAS for violating freedom and democracy and being a threat against the international peace and security, Cuba is almost begged to be reinstated to the OAS, and after rejecting to come back it goes to the Panama summit in command of the Latin American countries against the US, and with the express recognition of the latter. That enshrines the leadership of Latin America in the hands of Castro and Cuba. What follows after the Panama summit is the opening of relations between the US and Cuba and the visit of the American president to the island. Definitely, organized crime's greatest moment of political triumph over democracy.

During this 21st century, Latin America has had two clear leaderships. First Hugo Chávez, who acted as the undisputed leader because he was handling money and privilege, with Fidel Castro as a sort of oracle in Havana, to whom all heads of State and government paid homage visits. The death of Chavez, who at some point must be the subject of a serious historical investigation due to the extraordinary benefit and power that it inherited to Cuba, switched power to the hands of the Castros from Venezuela to Cuba, until they entered a new crisis.

I truly believe that Latin America does not have a leadership today, and that a fight is being waged that is no longer the confrontation that I narrated in my book on the two Americas, between dictatorship and democracy. There are still two Americas that confront each other, but now they are one democratic America, and another one controlled by a criminal organization. The confrontation translates as permanent conspiracy, threats against the security and integrity of the States, terrorism, drug trafficking, human rights violations, crimes against humanity, crimes against nature, devastation of natural and protected resources and more.

That criminal Castrochavista America, which is not political in nature, is the target of this book in which, through case studies, analysis, columns, essays and data taken from the objective reality, I intend to demonstrate that the Castrochavismo that today controls Cuba, Venezuela, Bolivia and Nicaragua under the guise of dictatorships, electoral dictatorships or dictatorships of transnational organized crime, is a criminal entity that must be isolated from politics and treated as transnational organized crime within the framework of the Palermo Convention[132] and other international standards, without the immunities or privileges inherent to the heads of State or government.

Castrochavismo wielded the leadership of Latin America with Chávez, and then with the Castros, but they fall into crises because the people start having problems; because the statist and criminal model of these regimes leads to crises, and they are poor administrators with hyper corruption. They have dissipated the wealth of Venezuela; the high prices of raw materials that helped them for a while are gone; people are fighting for their freedom and internal conflicts appear, so they'd lose control of much of the region. They already lost control of the OAS as well.

The Castrochavista dictatorships are in critical situation today, making great efforts to survive as they follow the model of the Cuban dictatorship, that boasts about 60 years in power. This is a new scenario, a defensive scenario in which Castrochavismo, instead of keeping up its expansion, is exhausted, is questioned, and has been downgraded to the control of Cuba, Venezuela, Bolivia and Nicaragua. The latest of these losses was Ecuador, a country that thanks to the vision of the current president Lenin Moreno, candidate and successor to dictator Correa, has clearly left that group.

Castrochavista dictatorships are in crisis but far from defeated. They are called out as regimes that violate human rights, have no rule of law, do not allow division or independence of public powers, and are narco States and creators of poverty. To remain in power, they apply a uniform strategy: "resisting at all costs, destabilizing democracies, politicizing their situation and negotiating." The strategic leadership still belongs to the Cuban dictatorship, which has converted the exercise of organized crime from the

---

[132] United Nations, year 2000. United Nations Convention against Transnational Organized Crime (Palermo Convention), a multilateral treaty.

power of the State into a methodology of social and political control, expanding such practices (operated by Cuban personnel) to Venezuela, Nicaragua and Bolivia,.

The first element of its strategy, of "retention of power at all costs," can be seen in Nicaragua and how many people they have tortured, imprisoned and killed last year; in Venezuela, where the same has been happening for years; in Cuba's never-ending repression and political prisoners. Look at Bolivia, from where the president of the human rights assembly has just reported that there are 131 uninvestigated deaths attributed to the government and more than 100 political prisoners; while the United Nations High Commissioner for Refugees (UNHCR), reports more than 1,200 Bolivians exiled in Brazil, Peru, the United States, Spain and Paraguay.

The second element of their strategy is to "destabilize democracies," for which they conspire against those who accuse them and against governments that defend democracy. They conspire from Argentina to the US; there is a conspiracy in Peru, there is a conspiracy in Panama, there is a conspiracy in Colombia, where now the FARC is resuming their armed struggle; there is a conspiracy in Brazil, because they have a lot of money to exacerbate genuine claims that may lie in a society and turn them into actions of political destabilization that they then use to negotiate and extort. The destabilizing actions range from false news and character assassination of leaders that they portray as right-wing, to criminal acts of terrorism, kidnappings and narco guerrillas.

The third element of their strategy is to "politicize their situation and their criminal acts" and that has to do with this book. When the dictatorships in Cuba, Venezuela, Bolivia, Nicaragua, improperly imprison a citizen, when they torture them, when they even kill them, they call it defense of the revolution. It is not murder, it is not torture, it is not crime, it is to defend the revolution, and so they build their causes of criminal justification. These four dictatorships are narco-States and, to justify themselves, they argue that "drug trafficking is an instrument of struggle for the liberation of the people", repeating and refining the fallacy that began with Fidel Castro in the 60s, repeated by Che Guevara, and proclaimed by Evo Morales in 2016 at the United Nations, saying that "the fight against drug trafficking is an instrument of imperialism to oppress the peoples". That is to say, there is a justification in revolutionary terms for any crime, criminally in Castrochavismo. If there's any doubt, watch out what just happened to a criminal drug dealer who fled from Colombia to Venezuela: Jesús Santrich has claimed that he is being persecuted by the right, and by the *tremendously fierce* government of Colombia. The real thing is that this is a criminal who belongs in jail, because even after signing the peace treaty he was trafficking drugs, he was filmed and photographed doing it, and there should be no more truthful evidence than that. How about the bosses of the Colombian narco guerrilla ELN, enjoying Cuban protection? This third element of Castrochavismo's strategy, politicizing their crimes, serves to ensure that when they kill anyone they can say that they are defending the revolution, when they torture someone they'd say they are defending the popular process of people's liberation and so on. They commit new crimes every day to preserve the impunity of the previous ones and keep their hold on power.

The fourth element of the Castrochavista strategy is to "negotiate." They negotiate in order to gain time, demoralize the adversary, pass bills to their allies or extort money from third States to gain their support or at least neutralize them. They capably mix these four elements and that's how they survive.

Among the many cases proving that the dictatorships of Cuba, Venezuela, Bolivia and Nicaragua are nothing political, but pure organized crime, those of Cuba stand out. They cover the "trafficking of Cuban slave doctors" with the alibi that it is a remarkable example of internationalism and cooperation for the liberation of the peoples, when in fact, far from being real social assistance for the Brazilians, Bolivians, Ecuadoreans, Venezuelans, or people wherever they send doctors, it is genuine 21st century slavery. For each doctor or any other professional, the Cuban dictatorship keeps more than 80% of paid salaries. The poor doctors are slaves whose family members are kept hostage in Cuba; they have to surrender their passports. And everything is facilitated by the Pan American Health Organization, at the service of a crime typified and condemned by the second annex to the Palermo Convention.

In Brazil, thanks to a decision by President Bolsonaro, the human trafficking with slave doctors hired to the "Mais Médicos" program has ceased, but there are still doctors and other types of Cuban slaves in Bolivia, Venezuela, Nicaragua and another six dozen countries. That is organized crime, but it continues to receive such legitimacy as if we were dealing with a political event, a relationship between governments to traffic people, even an act of cooperation, instead of clearly calling it out as a criminal act.

Other crimes of Castrochavismo that are "public and notorious facts" are drug trafficking, simulation and electoral fraud; torture and murder; political prisoners and exiles; attacks on freedom of the press; corruption and illicit enrichment, with family members and their entourage exhibiting their ill-gained fortunes around the world; criminal association to launder resources from criminal activities; confiscations of private property (we must remember that private property is a human right proclaimed by Article 19 of the Universal Declaration of Human Rights). All of these and so on is plain crime, it is not political.

I insist that "political" means based on respect for the "rule of law," which is simply that "no one is above the law,"; on the temporality of public service; on accountability and public responsibility, where you can take on an adversary. But organized crime has no adversaries, it has enemies, and the difference between an adversary and an enemy is that the former is defeated or persuaded, whereas the latter is eliminated, and this can explain the number of crimes that Castrochavismo perpetrates in the Americas.

The criminal handling these dictatorships undertake of offenses against the freedoms of the people can be appreciated in Nicaragua, where the regime takes prisoners, negotiates their freedom and releases the prisoners just to take them back, managing such a dynamic for intimidation purposes. The same has been the case in Venezuela, where there are hundreds of political prisoners. Castrochavista dictatorships have manipulated justice as a mechanism for persecution and political repression, another area of their criminal activity. With this, in addition to demonstrating that there is no division or independence of powers, they violate virtually every right. The "legalization of political repression" is another concept resulting from the criminal nature of Castrochavismo.

One of the examples closest to me of what organized crime action means is currently being carried out in my country, Bolivia, where Castrochavismo repeats an *iter criminis* already perpetrated in Venezuela and Nicaragua. *Iter criminis* means "the process of development of a crime", it is the "path that an offender goes through from the moment he intends to perpetrate a crime, through the preparation and carrying out of the intermediate steps of the crime until the criminal act is completed."

In Bolivia they will hold elections on October 20th. Castrochavista elections are electoral dictatorship, where you vote but you do not elect. A brief summary of the crimes that have been committed and continue to be committed: Evo Morales supplanted the political constitution of the State and liquidated the Republic of Bolivia in 2009, by establishing a constitution that gives birth to a Plurinational State (Spanish: plurinacional). In that constitution, founded on falsifications, massacres and exile that facilitated its approval, he states that he can only be reelected once, only once; then in 2009 he is immediately elected, and when that mandate expired in 2014, he goes back to re-election. He can no longer be reelected, but Morales asks his Constitutional Court for an interpretation, and it comes back saying that, having been the Republic of Bolivia extinguished, and the Plurinational State been born in 2009, Evo

144

Morales has only been elected once in the Plurinational State; that is, this is his first reelection so he can run again in 2014. That is to say they criminally simulate that Morales never made it to the presidency of the Republic of Bolivia, thus committing a crime of prevarication and falsehood, of material, ideological falsehood, an act of genuine organized crime.

We are not talking about politics, because if it were political there would be a constitutional body, a supreme court, to exercise constitutional control and to say that it cannot be allowed because it does not meet the principles of the "rule of law." But in organized crime, judgments are characterized by prevarication, and the judges are mere instruments, dependents of power and at its service.

But the criminal chain continues. After being illegally re-elected in 2014, Evo Morales calls a referendum seeking indefinite reelection and, despite fraud and manipulation, on February 21st, 2016, he loses. Bolivia said NO. This is summarized today as "21F Bolivia said NO". But such a result only marks the beginning of a new series of crimes covered by the political alibi of a supposed "change process" in Bolivia.

Under these conditions and to run for reelection on October 20th, Evo Morales orders his Constitutional Court and his Supreme Electoral Tribunal to perpetrate a new prevarication with judgments and rulings that enabled him, with the argument that "being a candidate is a human right," thus ignoring the mandate of Article 32.2 of the same American Convention on Human Rights, that they claim to apply, which mandates that "the rights of each person are limited by the rights of others, by the safety of all and by the just demands of the common good, in a democratic society."[133]

---

[133] American Convention on Human Rights. Pact of San Jose, Costa Rica, November 7 to 22, 1969

So the crimes go on and on in the so-called electoral process in Bolivia, with the presence of "functional candidates" that enable the usurper candidate to sustain the farce of the regime and weaken the defense of the return to democracy. Still, the people is fighting back and preparing a "civil resistance."

The peoples of Cuba, Venezuela, Nicaragua and Bolivia are fighting against the dictatorships that oppress them, but what they are taking on is not a local or national oppressor, but a transnational enemy, united around the goal of retaining power indefinitely as the best mechanism for impunity.

As a transnational organized crime structure Castrochavismo is a very powerful usurper with a lot of money, a legion of criminal armed forces, control of many media and many specialized mercenaries at its service, which puts the peoples they oppress in a true and extreme "defenseless condition."

I reiterate that the axis of confrontation today is between Democracy and Castrochavismo, meaning organized crime that has taken political power. It is not an ideological confrontation; it is a matter of survival in which a way of life based on freedom and justice is at stake.

If we determine to call things by their names and treat them accordingly, we will recover democracy and republican life more quickly in Cuba, Venezuela, Bolivia and Nicaragua and we will be able to keep it in the rest of the countries. As long as there are dictatorships there will be no peace or security in the Americas.

Bolivia, a new model insurgency for the 21st century: from Mao back to Lenin

David E. Spencer and Hugo Achá

ABSTRACT

In Bolivia, a brilliantly executed insurgency was carried out between 1995 and 2005, so much so that few perceived it as such. Its most important characteristic was its correct evaluation of the relative correlation of forces and application of the right combination of all forms of struggle. This was possible because of its pragmatism. Though not bound by ideological dogmatism, it nonetheless displayed a deep understanding of insurgency and revolutionary theory. This allowed adaptation and evolution in a changing context. The main form of struggle was not military violence, although it was not absent, but rather violent social protest funded by drug trafficking proceeds. The strategy thus neutralized traditional counterinsurgency models, because it made it difficult to apply coercive force as the enemy was not clearly identifiable. its success in Bolivia means that the emergence of a new model of insurgency, one still built upon the popular mobilization of people's war but more attuned to new global realities, is a reality.

This article was published at *Small Wars & Insurgencies*, 2017 Vol 28, No 3, 629-660

Just as the US and its allies have developed increasingly sophisticated models of counterinsurgency, so the enemies of the West have also developed adapted models of insurgency designed to frustrate and defeat these efforts. One such model was successfully executed by the Coca Growers (referred to hereafter as Cocaleros) in Bolivia between 1995 and 2003, which was consolidated with the election of Evo Morales at the end of 2005. It is important to understand this model, because it breaks with many of the methods we currently associate with insurgency, yet fully applies the tried

147

and true principles long identified by revolutionary theorists such as Mao, but perhaps even more so, Lenin.

Ironically, the 2005 electoral triumph of Evo Morales and his Movement to Socialism (MAS) party would not on its face be considered as the product of an insurgency, but this article will attempt to show that it was indeed an insurgency — a brilliantly conceived and executed uprising that applied the principles of insurgency to maximum advantage in the context of Turn of the Century Bolivia.[134] Elements of this model are now showing up in other countries in the region. The Cocaleros were undogmatic in their approach, although they were guided by principles they had learned from the miners' unions. They adapted their method5 over time, keeping what worked and very rapidly discarding what didn't. This application of principles combined with pragmatism is significant, because much of the West's counter-insurgency apparatus is intended to implement certain predictable methodologies. These, though, are neutralized by this new model, because its components make government capabilities inappropriate or even irrelevant.

To summarize, the Bolivian insurgency model was based on the following five lines of effort:

(1) Violence was limited but not unimportant. It was employed judiciously in two principal ways: first, guerrilla warfare was employed to protect the Cocaleros' main source of income, coca production, and was strictly limited to the drug producing areas (i.e. the Chapare). Second, flying columns accompanied the social protests during key events to employ selective violence to produce incidents between the anti-riot forces and the crowds to up the ante, embolden the masses, and delegitimize the government. Every attempt was made to keep the use of violence 'invisible' in the sense that in the Chapare it was attributed to

---

[134] Transition between the twentieth and the twenty-first century.

individuals and amorphous 'drug traffickers' reacting to counter-drug operations, and during the protests it was attributed to marchers reacting to government repression, rather than as a deliberate and systematic line of effort by the Cocalero organization and its allies. Cocaleros and their allies were portrayed as innocents exercising their constitutional rights. The limited and selective use of violence made it politically difficult, and even undesirable (because it seemed so extreme), for the government to declare the Cocaleros as insurgents. Yet this played into Cocalero hands, because by not doing so, successive administrations failed to expose the real danger of the Cocaleros and their intention to overthrow the Bolivian government.

(2) Money gathered from quotas on coca production and trafficking was used to finance the violence, the social protests, and eventually the creation, expansion, and activities of a political party. It was also used to buy off key opposition individuals or groups. The steady flow of money was potent and gave the Cocaleros cohesion, staying power, and the ability to manipulate their environment.

(3) Social protests were the main 'visible' effort of the insurgency. These were neither random nor spontaneous. Each sub-component of the unions known as a *Senda* (trail) was assigned a quota of marchers to participate in the protests for a determined period of time (called being, *En comisión*), usually 18 months. This maneuver force was led by a highly trained cadre of junior and intermediate leaders operating under a very efficient chain of command. During their' commissions, marchers were paid a salary by the Federations and their families were looked after. This professional core of Cocalero protesters allied itself with other social groups such as the labor unions, miners, and the indigenous organizations. This allowed them to mobilize rapidly around just about every anti-government

cause and to carry out prolonged marches that kept the country in perpetual crisis.

(4) A legal political party was formed that participated in the normal political process. This political party offered itself as the solution to the social chaos that in reality was its own creation and served to legally consolidate the gains obtained via illegal and illegitimate means.

(5) An information campaign aided by some mostly European NGOs presented the unrest not as a struggle to perpetuate the narcotics trade but rather as a struggle for long-suppressed indigenous rights. Thus, confronting the Cocaleros became politically incorrect, synonymous with repressing impoverished, indigenous peoples.

Truong Chinh developed the concept that has been translated into English as the 'War of Interlocking.' In Latin America, this term has been translated as the 'Combination of All Forms of Struggle' (*combinación de todas las formas de lucha*). It posits that to take power, all lines of action or effort occur simultaneously. All forms include legal political struggle, illegal political struggle, and various modes of violent, economic, social, and informational (and other) action. Not only do all occur simultaneously but none are rejected. The level of effort of each, or the form or forms of struggle that predominate at any given moment, depends on the relative correlation of forces between the insurgents and the government in time and space. As this correlation of forces shifts, so must the predominant forms of struggle if the insurgency wishes to progress towards victory. Insurgencies that are inflexible in their approaches tend to lose, because they are unable to adapt to the shifting correlations of forces. Their enemies figure out their patterns and crush them.

In twentieth and early twenty-first century insurgency, various forms of violence have generally predominated, because, as the insurgents claim, legal forms of political competition have been exhausted and the only way forward to compete politically is through violence. Within violence, there are various methods of action which change as the correlation of force shifts. When the state is strong and the insurgents are weak, violence tends to be more irregular, and the organizations that perpetuate the violence are more dispersed. As the state weakens, and the insurgency is able to mobilize more resources, the methods of violence tend to become more regular and the form of organization more concentrated. Should the state fail to respond adequately, the insurgency can become a regular or nearly regular army and eventually march into the nation's capital to establish a new government. However, should the government recover its strength, to survive, the insurgency will drop back to more irregular action and dispersed forms of organization. In theory then, insurgencies occur in wave-like patterns as the correlation of forces waxes and wanes, rather than in strictly linear patterns as some have represented. This allows the insurgency to continually act but still conserve its core forces and avoid defeat.

These patterns of rising and falling intensities of violence are what most insurgency analysts focus on. This is because in the West, insurgency is largely seen as a type of warfare, and while insurgents would not dispute that they are carrying out a form of warfare, most insurgencies think of their struggle as a form of politics with warfare being but one of the ways to achieve their political ends. The ultimate goal is to replace the existing regime with a new one. Therefore, there is much more depth to insurgency than just the military or violence line of struggle, even if this is often the predominant line of effort.

In theory, insurgencies can maintain this wave-like pattern of military activity indefinitely if they have the proper depth in other forms of struggle. The Vietnamese called this concept *dau tranh*, which in English means 'struggle.'[135] The Vietnamese maintained that the military struggle could be continually regenerated as long

---

[135] The seminal source on this subject remains Pike, PAVN.

as the political struggle was maintained at a sufficient level. To the Vietnamese, the political struggle was essentially all of the forms of struggle other than the military struggle combined: political legal, political illegal, social, economic, informational, diplomatic, and so forth.[136] Thus, for counterinsurgency, it is necessary but not sufficient to defeat military *dau tranh*. Sufficiency is only achieved when the counterinsurgency also defeats the political struggle. For even if temporarily militarily defeated, the intact political infrastructure will eventually regenerate the military effort.

Since insurgency and counterinsurgency have largely been a military concern in the West, dealing with the non-military side of insurgency is precisely where Western nations are weak. We have built very sophisticated military capabilities to defeat irregular military forces, but the same sophistication does not exist in the non-military arena. There is certainly theoretical understanding of the need for this non-military struggle, but implementation has been severely lacking perhaps due to the military's sub-optimal preparation for this mission and the civilian agencies' lack of consciousness and incentives to perform this task. Without completely discarding the military struggle, it is into this gap that new forms of insurgency are stepping.

Ironically, in focusing on the non-military struggle, they are returning to very old roots, specifically the ideas and theory developed by Lenin. For Lenin, the principal struggle was always political. The military struggle was auxiliary to the political struggle. It could reach very advanced levels of violence, even to regular war, but it was always auxiliary and secondary to the political effort. Though Mao's synthesis, due to its symbiosis of the military and the political, is often interpreted as akin to guerrilla war on steroids (with good behavior thrown in), nothing could be further from the totality of the approach. This was not different

---

[136] This is not unlike the Chinese concept of 'political warfare'; see Marks, Counterrevolution in China.

from what we have previously discussed with respect to the Vietnamese.[137] It was the Cubans with foco theory who subordinated the political effort to the military vanguard.

Still, Mao in many ways was captive to his time and place. Military effort achieved primacy in the seizure of power. Lenin was theoretically more flexible and wrote:

> Under no circumstances does Marxism confine itself to the forms of struggle possible and in existence at the given moment only, recognizing as it does that new forms of struggle, unknown to the participants of the given period, inevitably arise as the given social situation, changes. In this respect Marxism learns, if we may so express it, from mass practice, and makes no claim whatever to teach the masses forms of struggle invented by 'systematizers' in the seclusion of their studies.[138]

In other words, Lenin advocated that revolutionaries should embrace what produced results, and that they adapt and evolve as the situation evolved. He also wrote:

> Marxism demands an absolutely historical examination of the question of the forms of struggle. To treat this question apart from the concrete historical situation betrays a failure to understand the rudiments of dialectical materialism. At different stages of economic evolution, depending on differences in political, national-cultural, living and other conditions, different forms of struggle come to the fore and become the principal forms of struggle; and in connection with this, the secondary, auxiliary forms of struggle undergo change in their turn. To attempt to answer yes or no to the question whether any particular means of struggle should be used, without making a detailed examination of the concrete situation of the given movement at the given stage of its development, means completely to abandon the Marxist position.[139]

The Bolivian Cocaleros did this often, consistently and brilliantly, which the following narrative demonstrates.

---

[137] See Marks, *Maoist People's War in Post-Vietnam Asia.*

[138] Lenin, *Guerrilla Warfare*

[139] Ibid.

Evolution of the Bolivian model

In 1980, Roberto Suarez — the world's first king of cocaine, who was later eclipsed by Pablo Escobar — financed a military coup by General Luis Garcia Meza. For the next two years, the Bolivian government became known for its close relationship to drug trafficking, earning the nickname of the 'narco-state.' Under the narco-state, the government actively collaborated in the expansion of coca cultivation in the Chapare, a jungle area in the Department of Santa Cruz. At the same time, assisted by the Argentine military government, it conducted a heavy crack-down on militant leftists. Under international condemnation, unable to meet its economic goals and facing a miners' strike that took the country to the verge of civil war, the military accelerated the transition to democracy, allowing Hernan Siles Suazo, originally elected in 1980, to assume the presidency. The military coup had been launched to prevent his inauguration as he was considered a Marxist by the coup leaders.

Siles Suazo inherited a poor economic situation, but the socialist economic policies he implemented only accelerated a more severe economic crisis. By 1984, the Bolivian mines — until then Bolivia's main source of revenue — were economically broken. This was due to a combination of exhaustion of the mines, reduction of the price of Bolivian minerals, and economically unsustainable labor costs.

The mining unions that were behind much of this lack of sustainable labor costs had been formed in the early twentieth century. By the 19305, they were dominated by Marxist thought and organization, which gave them a class struggle world-view, strategic thinking, planning, organization, and discipline, as well as a tradition of semi-violent militant struggle. The latter was reinforced when veterans of the Chaco War returned to the mines after 1935, bringing their personal side-arms with them, and, more importantly, experience in a war that was considered by many to be the first modern war in Latin America. The armed miners combined with other groups carried out the 1952 revolution through the National Revolutionary Movement (MNR). The MNR briefly jailed, retired, or suspended the army officer corps and organized workers and peasants into militias,[140] distributing to them surplus weapons from the Chaco War. These weapons have remained in the hands of the workers and peasants ever since. This meant that social protests in Bolivia usually involved violence, particularly when the miners went on strike, because they carried the conviction that they could defeat the security forces. In addition to their firearms, they also carried sticks of dynamite, which they were fond of tossing at their foes.

When the mines broke — to avoid sustained violence — the government offered to each miner a severance check of approximately USD 2000.00. A large proportion of the ex-miners took their severance pay and migrated to the Chapare region, where they acquired plots of land and began growing coca. Coca production soon expanded to some 98,850 acres.

Yet the new democratic governments were not as tolerant of cocaine trafficking as the previous military regime had been. In August 1983, the government signed an agreement to receive US counternarcotics assistance to reduce drug trafficking to the United States from the Chapare. The United States trained a 300-man police unit, the Unidad Móvil Policial para Areas Rurales (UMOPAR), also known as the Leopards.[141] The UMOPAR along with 1500 Bolivian troops entered the Chapare in mid-1984 and began to conduct eradication operations. In response, the coca-growing peasants organized unions along the lines of the model

---

[140] Composed mostly of Chaco War veterans, therefore combat hardened compared to the regular army conscripts.

[141] Mendel, *Counterdrug Strategy Illusive Victory*: 74-87

they brought with them from the mines. Eventually, the unions would represent 35,000 families grouped into 6 Federations which actively resisted the eradication efforts of the troops. The military was unprepared for such a strong peasant response and soon withdrew its forces.[142]

Blast furnace

In July 1986, the United States launched Operation Blast Furnace in cooperation with the Bolivian government. This combined operation involved operational troops from the Bolivian police and army with logistical and transportation support from the US military, to include six Black Hawk helicopters and 160 pilots and maintenance personnel to provide air mobility to the Bolivian troops. The operation lasted four months and although the results were short-lived, they did cause the price of coca to drop below the cost of production for the duration of the operation.

This also consolidated the power of the coca growers' federation of unions, which in the best miner union tradition, organized violent mass protests against the counter-narcotics operations, one of which managed to expel 150 Bolivian and US troops from the town of Santa Ana de Yacuma in the Beni at the end of the operation.[143] They also discovered that the mass protests in the Chapare had an unintended strategic consequence. The two national highways between the breadbasket of eastern Bolivia and the capital, La Paz, ran through the Chapare. The protests on the roads caused scarcity of food and other items in La Paz, which then caused general dissatisfaction with the government. Government concessions followed to prevent greater uprisings in the capital. This would become a key component in the insurgent strategy.

---

[142] Ibid.

[143] Ibid.

In this way Blast Furnace both set the pattern of US-Bolivian government cooperation and the pattern of resistance to these operations by the Cocaleros. Each side absorbed lessons learned and prepared for the future. On the one hand, the relative success of Blast Furnace caused the United States to develop plans for more sustained and better resourced counter-narcotics operations; on the other, the Cocalero Federations began making plans to up the ante and more effectively resist the counter-narcotics operations.

Law 1008

The Bolivian government passed the 'Coca and Controlled Substances Regimen' or Law 1008 in July 1988. This law identified cocaine as an illegal substance. It identified and controlled all substances that could be employed as precursor chemicals for the production of cocaine. However, it differentiated between coca for traditional use, which remained legal, and coca grown for cocaine, deemed illegal.[144] It established an office to organize and manage counternarcotics operations, the National Council against Illicit Drug Trafficking, known by its Spanish acronym, CONALTID.[145]

It divided the coca growing regions of the country into three categories. Designated as a site of legitimate activity was a zone in the Yungas of approximately 29,700 acres of coca where traditional, low-alkaloid, coca was grown. This was used for the traditional chewing leaves, teas, and other products that have long been sold openly in Bolivia. An excess transition zone, where coca was being grown for illegal purposes, but where crops were already being

---

[144] The variant of coca for the production of cocaine has been bred for this purpose and has a much higher alkaloid content. It cannot be chewed or used to make traditional teas. Thus, the Cocalero argument that it was being grown for traditional reasons, often repeated in the international press, was spurious.

[145] Consejo Nacional contra el Tráfico Ilícito de Drogas.

substituted for a variety of legal and legitimate crops, was exempted from coercive action. A third zone of illicit production, mostly in the Chapare, was designated for aggressive eradication and alternative development.[146]

Law 1008 became the bane of the Cocaleros' existence, and abrogating this law became their main political objective and the justification of their insurgency. Violence in the form of military action was always considered a viable option, and the Cocaleros prepared for the possibility of open warfare. They developed ties to regional and international terrorist organizations and began importing advisers to teach them methods of irregular warfare. In particular, they were interested in techniques for the manufacture and employment of explosive devices. To instruct them, they brought in advisers from Sendero Luminoso in Peru, FARC and ELN in Colombia, and the Basque ETA. However, they did not limit themselves to this method. To develop a pool of militarily trained personnel, they ordered their young men to fulfill their national military service obligation, the evasion of which was nearly a national sport in other sectors of society. Favored was volunteering for service in Bolivia's elite units, such as the Parachute regiment, the Ranger regiment, or the Satinadores.[147] After returning from service, these men were organized into a paramilitary organization known as the Reservation Guard (*Guardia de Reserva*), as part of the Chapare is supposedly a national forest. Later, this force was renamed the Syndicate Police. From then on, armed resistance to police and army counterdrug operations became increasingly violent and featured ambushes, the employment of snipers, assaults, and improvised explosive devices (IEDs). It was not difficult to obtain weapons as the Bolivian military suffered from notorious corruption. Officers and NCOs willingly sold

---

[146] CICAD, Evaluación de los Compromisos plasmados en el Plan Dignidad.

[147] An archaic Spanish term meaning trail blazer or pathfinder.

weapons and ammunition, particularly to men returning home after military service. While most recruits had little money personally, their contacts invariably did.[148]

Another important discovery for the Cocaleros was the self-imposed ethical and philosophical restraints of US-supported operations. Americans were highly sensitive to the poor social conditions in Bolivia, hence their constant concern to offer social programs and alternative development initiatives along with the counter-narcotics operations. They also reacted strongly to the presence and suffering of women and children amongst protesters. Finally, US and European media, heavily influenced by their own NGOs, had a significant impact on the policy debate in their own countries and the international pressure brought to bear on the Bolivian government. Playing this card, as would also be done by the Zapatistas in Chiapas, became an important component in the overall anti-government effort.

Additionally, the Cocaleros quickly came to the conclusion that they needed to influence national policy through political participation. The first efforts involved offering money to existing political parties to represent them and allow them to place electoral candidates. The Cocaleros were not particularly concerned about the ideological orientation of the party, and they approached several disparate parties. They were universally rejected, except by the leftist Izquierda Unida Party (PIU). Joining with PIU allowed them to participate in legal electoral politics and obtain some success, as four Cocalero representatives, among them Evo Morales, were elected to Congress in 1989.

Meanwhile, as Bolivia went through a series of economic and social crises, coca cultivation began to expand. In 1986, coca crops were estimated at 100,360 acres. By 1993, they had reached

---

[148] Interview with anonymous source who did his military service in the Ranger Regiment from 1990 to 1992, 23 September 2014.

147, 800 acres.[149] At this time, coca was grown in Bolivia and Peru and then flown to Colombia for processing in local cocaine labs. However, the Colombians subsequently discovered that certain variants of coca grew well in their soil and stopped importing the leaves from outside. Colombians also took the refining process to Bolivia and Peru, where the locals began to process the leaves in their own countries because it was much more efficient to transport coca base or cocaine powder than to transport leaves. Subsequently, the trafficking from Bolivia became more direct to the final markets, and profits increased for the Cocaleros. By 1997, Bolivia was exporting 250 metric tons of cocaine per year with a street value of USD 7.5 billion.[150]

Cocalero strategy

The Cocalero Federations made strategic decisions through conferences and plenums, following the Marxist doctrine for labor unions. Conferences are held to establish strategy; plenums are held to make course adjustments to the strategic plan. At a 1995 Conference, a faction of the leadership, to include the President of the Six Federations, Evo Morales, proposed that the Cocaleros launch classic guerrilla warfare to overthrow the Bolivian government in order to put a stop to US-supported counternarcotics operations. Their view was that in the end, this was the only way to ultimately defend coca.[151] The chief political adviser for the Cocaleros, a long-time veteran from the miners' movement, Filemon Escobar, acknowledged that the conditions for guerrilla warfare in the Chapare were far more favorable than Ñancahuasú had been for Che Guevara in 1967. However, he warned the Cocaleros that despite this, an all-out guerrilla war would only attract the wrath

---

[149] CICAD, Evaluación, 6.

[150] Government of the Republic of Bolivia, Memoria, 380.

[151] Rodríguez "Evitar la Confrontación"

of the US, and the movement would eventually be crushed.[152] Instead, he advocated a more Leninist approach of continuing to emphasize mass protests to push the rest of the country to the brink of collapse, accompanied by the creation of a Cocalero-controlled party, which he called the 'political instrument,' to participate in legal electoral politics.

After debating the merits of different approaches, the Cocalero leadership largely accepted Escobar's proposal. It kept the hawks within the fold, though, by approving the use of organized violence to resist to the counter-narcotics operations in the Chapare. This pacified the hawks, who included Evo Morales, because they continued to develop their fighting force for the day when it would eventually be used. They were extremely skeptical about the possibility of the Federation ever making significant gains through the legal political system and wanted to be ready to implement open warfare when the other options had been exhausted.[153] In this way, the Cocaleros were always prepared to implement much greater violence.

Lenin's approach to strategy is clearly evident. In his 1906 essay, 'Lessons of the Moscow Uprising,' Lenin discusses the internal debates his party had over the merits of the armed struggle versus unarmed forms of political struggle. It is clear that Lenin's view of insurgency contemplated a progression starting with street protests that, because of state intransigence and repression, would inevitably progress to barricades and end in an armed uprising. While the main action might be protests, the communists could not reject the option of armed struggle, and in fact needed to be wholly prepared for it.[154] The question was not in accepting or rejecting the use of armed struggle, rather the art of how and when to apply it. Lenin

---

[152] Ibid.

[153] Ibid.

[154] Lenin, *Lessons of the Moscow Uprising.*

called this moment, 'the fusion of terrorism and the mass movement,' but this fusion needed to take place as part of a process of 'sanely and coolly weighing the conditions under which they would become possible.'[155] Until that day, they needed to intensively prepare. Lenin advocated that this preparation not only involve training and gathering weapons but also 'separate armed actions, such as attacks by armed squads on the police and on troops during public meetings, or on prisons, government offices, etc.'[156] This is almost exactly what the Cocaleros did.

Plan Dignity

The Cocalero approach was severely tested during the 1998-2001 government of Hugo Banzer who, supported by the United States, implemented Plan Dignidad (Plan Dignity), a comprehensive counter-narcotics plan with the slogan of 'Zero Cocaine.'[157] Much criticized in anti-government circles, the truth is that this plan nearly succeeded in defeating the Cocaleros and eradicating coca cultivation in the Chapare.

Upon taking office, President Banzer convened a National Dialogue with broad sectors of society. The consensus supported completely eradicating drug trafficking from Bolivia to comply with the 1988 United Nations Declaration on Combating Drug Trafficking, to alleviate the impact on consumer nations, and to clean the image of Bolivia abroad.[158] Restoring dignity to Bolivia's name is why Banzer's plan was so-named.

---

[155] Lenin, *A Militant Agreement for the Uprising.*

[156] Lenin, *Congress of the R.S.D.L.X*

[157] Cocalero sympathizers have often portrayed this slogan as 'Zero Coca,' but traditional coca crops and coca uses were protected by Law 1008. Only coca for illicit uses was made illegal.

[158] Government of the Republic of Bolivia, Memoria, 375

Bolivia worked closely with the United States government to develop the counter-narcotics plan. The plan was composed of four pillars: (1) Alternative Development, (2) Prevention, (3) Eradication, and (4) Interdiction.[159] The objective was to completely eradicate illegal coca-cocaine production and trafficking from Bolivia by the end of the Banzer government and to incorporate the approximately 38,000 illicit coca producing families into the legal economy.[160] The US provided generous assistance on multiple levels. To help the country recover economically, the United States granted credit for development or food assistance exchanges, which significantly reduced Bolivia's foreign debt. In addition, the US put significant effort into developing effective alternative development projects. This was combined with robust counter-narcotics aid. Overall, the plan cost USD 952 million, of which USD 108 million (11%) was for eradication, USD 129 million (14%) for interdiction, USD 15 million (2%) for prevention, and USD 700 million (73%) for alternative development.[161] In FY2000, the US gave Bolivia USD 25 million counter-narcotics assistance and USD 85 million in alternative development assistance. For FY 2002, it provided USD 48.5 million in counter-narcotics aid and USD 74.46 million in alternative development aid. In FY 2003, Bolivia received USD 50 million in counter-narcotics assistance and USD 82.6 million in economic and social programs.[162] This aid was designed to offset the economic losses incurred, as it was estimated that drug trafficking injected approximately USD 600 million per year into the economy, up to 8% of the Bolivian Gross Domestic Product.[163]

---

[159] Ibid.

[160] Ibid., 378

[161] Defensor del Pueblo, Estudio de Violencia Intrafamiliar en Contextos de Violencia Generalizada, 17

[162] Storrs, Andean Regional Initiative (ARI), 15.

[163] Government of the Republic of Bolivia, op. cit., 378-9

The task force that carried out Plan Dignity was composed of the Counter Narcotics Struggle Special Forces (FELCN), the UMOPAR, the Task Force (Blue Devils (Navy), Red Devils [Air Force) and Green Devils [Army)), the Intelligence and Special Operations Group, the Chemical Substances Investigation Group, the Financial Investigative Unit, and the Drug Detecting Canine Center. Between 1997 and 2001, they carried out over 15,000 operations.[164]

Initially, Plan Dignity was not popular, and many Bolivians empathized with the plight of the Cocaleros, focusing on the economic misery caused by the eradication of coca. However, public opinion changed when the true nature of illicit cocaine and the criminals who controlled it became public.[165]

Notwithstanding, Plan Dignity was fiercely resisted, and violence was constant. While the figures are incomplete, between 1997 and 2003, the Andean Information Network (*Red Andina de Información*) reported that according to the Villa Tunari Public Defender (*Defensoría del Pueblo*) 35 Cocaleros were killed, 587 were seriously wounded, and 700 were jailed. During the same period and according to the same records, the military and police lost approximately 27 killed and 135 wounded. [166]This was probably low. Bolivian law prohibited spraying, so eradication had to be done by hand. As a result, security forces were exposed to Cocalero action. The Cocalero military wing harassed military units from the moment they entered the Chapare, attacking their patrol camps day and night with sharpshooters, only desisting when they left. They also carried out ambushes with IEDs. Often these were placed to prevent the removal of roadblocks, and automatic fire was sprayed after either the IEDs exploded or when the army sent

---

[164] Ibid., 381.

[165] Ibid.,380.

[166] Navia Gabriel and Pinto Cascán, "Mutilados y olvidados de Chapare."

forward men to deactivate the explosives.[167] In 2001, the anti-explosives unit of the Chapare Ecological Police recorded 109 harassment attacks, 39 ambushes, and the successful deactivation of 22 IEDs. It also recorded losses of seven killed and 50 wounded.[168] The International Campaign to Ban Landmines reported that the Ecological Police put their casualties in 2003 at 7 military killed and at least 91 wounded by all causes, mostly by IEDs.[169]

In addition to the ambushes, IEDs, and harassment attacks, the Cocaleros carried out simultaneous protests, blocking roads, and surrounding eradication camps to force the Army out. Occasionally, they would also attempt to overrun the camps both with violence and with protesting masses. However, Cocalero resistance was not only limited to the Chapare. In the year 2000, for example, they carried out a large march that blocked the National Highway between Cochabamba and Santa Cruz, causing estimated economic losses of more than USD 100 million.[170]

Evolution of the political instrument

In politics, the Cocaleros continued to evolve. While they had been incorporated into the Izquierda Unida Party (PIU), which happily accepted their money, they did not control it, and they discovered that outside of the Chapare, the cause of coca was rejected by the vast majority of the population. Building upon failed past experiences of miners' unions, they decided they needed to expand their

---

[167] Ibid.

[168] Guisela López, "Hay 100 desactivadores de cazabobos." *El Deber.* September 20, 2004.

[169] International Campaign to Ban Landmines, Landmine Monitoring Report 2004.

[170] Government of the Republic of Bolivia, op. cit., 379.

movement to represent more than just the Cocaleros.[171] For example, the cause of greater indigenous rights was widely accepted, not only by the majority of the national polity but especially by sectors of the international community interested in Bolivia. Based on this analysis, the Cocaleros very pragmatically shifted resources and manpower to aggressively coopt the indigenous rights movement and its leaders. This was not an unnatural shift since many of the Cocaleros were of partial or full indigenous blood, particularly of Aymara ancestry, and many were also either part of indigenous organizations (e.g. CSUTCB) or had relatives in them.

Cocalero penetration of indigenous organizations was not always well-received, but those who resisted were gradually marginalized or eliminated, and eventually the Cocaleros were able to dominate the most important indigenous groups. This was done through a systematic process of 'divide and conquer,' manipulating the relative lax discipline of the non-Cocalero organizations and exploiting the Cocaleros' comparatively vast wealth to influence the plenums of these organizations, particularly in getting Cocalero or pro-Cocalero candidates voted into leadership positions from which they could then steer the organization into making common cause with the Cocaleros.[172] In this way, they were able to dominate the CSUTCB and the miners' unions.

This broad national coalition then created the need for a legal national political movement, not controlled by others but fully controlled by the Cocaleros, which could represent all of these groups with a single political platform. The Cocalero leadership decided that it was no longer efficient to 'buy' political space from others. Instead, it would be better {and cheaper) to have a political party of their own.

---

[171] Rodríguez, "Evitar la Confrontración."

[172] http://www.bolpress.com/art.php?Cod=2014070403

When this decision was made, it was too close to the 1997 elections to go through the bureaucracy of creating a new party to participate in the elections, so they looked for an existing registered political party that they could take over. They found what they were looking for in the Movement to Socialism or MAS.[173] MAS was led by David Añez Pedraza, who had broken away from the Bolivian Socialist Falange in 1987 and formed the Unzaguista-Movement to Socialism or (MAS-U). In 1995, the party was registered in Cochabamba as the Movement to Socialism, dropping Unzaguista. The party was taken over by the Cocaleros for the 1997 elections. They essentially bought the party and chose David Añez as their candidate, because Evo Morales still lacked faith in electoral politics, convinced that armed struggle was the only way that power could be achieved.[174] Although the alliance of Cocaleros, Indigenous groups, and miners under the umbrella of MAS was too weak at the time to prevent the relentless forward progress of Plan Dignity, the Cocalero-controlled political instrument would pay off in the end by lending a veneer of institutional legitimacy to the insurgency.

At the time, Plan Dignity by most measures was highly successful. Net reduction of coca cultivation was approximately 70% between 1996 and 2001. Illegal coca production in the Yungas was nearly eliminated, and coca production in the Chapare was significantly reduced. Coca cultivation in Bolivia dropped steadily from 120,000 acres in 1995 to 36,000 acres by 2000.[175] Of the 96,100 acres of coca in the Chapare in 1997, by February 2001, only

---

[173] Movimiento al Socialismo

[174] See Note 38.

[175] Storrs, Andean Regional Initiative (ARI).

14,800 acres were left.[176] Cocaine exportation dropped to less than 70 metric tons, about 28% of its peak levels.[177]

The water war: a tipping point

At the Cocaleros' nadir, when the Banzer government was at the height of its success with Plan Dignity, an event occurred that began to resurrect the fortunes of the Cocalero movement. Cochabamba is a city with an abundant natural supply of water. However, for various reasons, it has an extremely inefficient water supply system. In the late 1990s, it was believed that the solution was privatization. A contract was signed in 1999 with International Waters Limited (IWL, a British subsidiary of the San Francisco-based Bechtel Company), which created a Bolivian company, Aguas del Tunari.[178] Part of the negotiations was an agreement that rates could increase as much as 35%. This was acceptable because of the capital investment that would be needed and the expectation that water services would be extended to most inhabitants and become much more efficient than before. However, when the rate hikes were implemented, rates went up by as much as 200-300%, figures which in many cases represented up to 25% of a resident's monthly income.[179] The resulting anger fed organization of protest.

The first protesters came from the informal water entrepreneurs who tapped natural wells and aquifers around Cochabamba. This group's livelihood was destroyed when the contract with IWI-gave Aguas del Turani rights over all sources of water in the region. The entrepreneurs created the Departmental Federation of

---

[176] See Note 17.

[177] See Not 31.

[178] Shultz and Draper, *Desafiando la Globalización*

[179] Barrero Cordero, *La Guerra del Agua en Cochabamba*, 94

Cochabamba Irrigators or FEDECOR. FEDECOR carried out the first relatively small protests in November 1999. Later, they united with the disenchanted consumers to form the 'Water and Life Co-ordinator' (hereafter referred to as the Water Coordinator), which sought the assistance of the Cocaleros to develop their plan of action.

Although severely battered by *Plan Dignity*, the Cocaleros still had money, organization, and experience. They had strong ties to Cochabamba through family and class, as many of the miners displaced in the 1980s who had not settled in the nearby Chapare had gone to Cochabamba city or its suburbs.

Many Cocalero children and youth from the Chapare studied in Cochabamba's schools and universities, so it was not hard to convince the Cocaleros to send cadre to participate in the protests. By January 2000, the Water Coordinator consisted of FEDECOR, the rural and urban teachers' unions, the Cochabamba factory workers, university students, the Chapare Cocaleros, and the Federation of Interdepartmental Transporters.[180]

This coalition carried out its initial protests during 11-13 January 2000, paralyzing the city. The protests ebbed and flowed through March, with cycles of protest, police repression, negotiation, and lulls. At the end of March, the government negotiating position began to weaken, and the Water Coordinator, sensing it was close to a tipping point, pulled out of negotiations and began what it called the 'popular consultation.' After getting 50,000 people to express in favor of rescinding the contract with Aguas del Tunari, the Water Coordinator called for a 'Final Battle.'[181] As in subsequent events, the Cocalero objective was no longer to gain

---

[180] Daroca Oller, "Protesta y Acción Social en Cochabamba," 7; also Humberto, "Bolivia", 48

[181] Ibid, 8

improved water services for a reasonable price; it was about defeating the government and increasing national political leverage. Not all of the coalition supported this 'final battle.' Many noted that the government was willing to negotiate a modification of the water contract that addressed the protesters' demands. The Civic Committee, Federation of Private Businesses, and Public Transportation Workers dropped their support for the Water Coordinator and accused the entity of now representing different interests. Indeed, they were correct. The Water Coordinator, by this time almost completely controlled by the Cocaleros, announced that it was no longer interested in negotiations, that it would only lift the protests if the Aguas del Tunari contract was completely rescinded.[182] Indefinite road blocks by Cocaleros and peasants in large numbers were implemented, and squads of young men violently invaded the offices of Aguas del Tunari, destroying and vandalizing the building and its offices.

The government reacted by sending military and police to break up the marches. They arrested the Water Coordinator leaders and used tear gas and rubber bullets to disperse the crowds. The Cocalero reaction was to intensify the protests. This coincided with a strike by the Police Special Group, the anti-riot police, demanding a 50% salary increase. One crowd tried to take over the headquarters of the Army 7th Division. To prevent this, some of the soldiers fired into the crowd, wounding several people, and a captain killed a 17-year-old youth. The image of the latter was repeatedly broadcast on TV until the government cut off the broadcasts, but the damage had already been done. The public was outraged, and the incident was used as a symbol to strengthen the mobilization even as military officers were reporting skilled tactics and maneuvering by small squads of men' who led the crowd and harassed the army and police. These reports were largely ignored outside the security forces. Another 30 persons were injured in the struggle, and then

---

[182] Ibid.

the Banzer government, seeing that it was facing politically unacceptable levels of violence, backed down and rescinded the Aguas del Tunari contract.[183]

The importance of the 'Water War' was that it was first time the Cocaleros participated in a social protest that was greater than their parochial concerns — and it had resulted in victory, not only against the Bolivian government, but against, in Cocalero minds, a 'neoliberal' international corporation, a perceived tool of 'Yankee Imperialism,' a foe similar in essence to the counter-narcotics policy. This was extremely important, because the victory signaled to them that 'the US' could be defeated. This experience taught the Cocaleros the strategic importance of making common cause with other social organizations and began a pattern of the Cocaleros seeking social conflict opportunities into which they could insert themselves. The objective, as in Mao's formulation of contradictions, was to rapidly escalate relatively minor controversies into major national social protests. For this very purpose, the different organizations banded together and formed the Mobilization Central Coordinator (Coordinadora de Movilizaciones Única Nacional) or COMUNAL to organize and coordinate national level protests whenever the opportunity arose.

Finally, it was the first time that the Cocaleros protested in a major city, and this taught them that the urban space, not the countryside, was the location for decisive battles. Demonstrating their trademark tactical flexibility, the Cocaleros quickly assimilated urban tactics into their essential toolbox. Still, though they noted the power and impact that protesting and operating in a major city had, they also realized that battle in a regional city was not decisive. For such a result, they had to conduct urban operations in the center of political power. Thus, they concluded they had to take the battle to the capital, La Paz.

---

[183] Ibid., 10-1.

End of Plan Dignity

Cocalero ability to join and take over protests led by other organizations soon manifested itself. The Teachers' Federation declared an indefinite national strike in support of instructors from Oruro, who began a March from Oruro to La Paz and organized protesters and hunger strikes in all of the major cities. COMUNAL joined the teachers and organized roadblocks along all of the country's major highways, particularly the east-west highways between Santa Cruz, Cochabamba, and La Paz. It also mobilized the CSUTCB and the COB to protest in the Altiplano, especially in and around Achacachi. What had started out as a teachers' protest was essentially taken over by Evo Morales and the Cocaleros in the Chapare and by Felipe Quispe in Achacachi.[184] The roads remained blocked for over a month in the Chapare, requiring military force to open them and disperse the protesters. Reportedly, even businessmen protested against the government, because the roadblocks were seriously affecting their enterprises.[185]

The government attempted to break the movement by negotiating separately with each of the groups, and it achieved what would be the last success of a democratic government in dealing with the Cocalero movement. On August 23, the CSUTCB signed a document of 70 points with the government and suspended the roadblocks in La Paz. Felipe Quispe, CSTUCB chief executive and the most influential indigenous leader of the day, declared that he was not against the national counternarcotics policy. Little did Quispe understand that he had just signed the end of his political career.

Outraged, Morales believed he could precipitate open rebellion and ordered the Cocalero columns to try to take the military Base

---

[184] Vargas, op. cit., 48-49

[185] Ledebur, *Coca y Conflicto en el Chapare*, 6; Vargas, op. cit., 49.

Verde Ill located 118 miles from Cochabamba and the eradication outposts of Loma Alta, Urkupina, Bolivar A, Bolivar B, and Isinuta. The military reported 'many but undetermined' casualties among the assaulting Cocaleros during the August 13-September 26 assaults. However, the Cocaleros only admitted the death of a single woman. On 27 September, the Cocalero movement took a number of journalists to Loma Alta, where they witnessed the 'protests,' a force of approximately 800 Cocaleros assaulting the military outpost. Right in front of their eyes, a Cocalero was hit by rifle fire and died.

Try as they might, the Cocaleros could not overrun the bases, and the military would not withdraw. Instead, Banzer ordered a huge mobilization of troops to force open all the highways in the country. Internal Cocalero documents about these events heavily criticized Morales, and some Cocaleros even demanded that he be removed from his position. A recommendation was made to shift focus from the counter-eradication effort to broader political action.

Yet the Cocaleros were closer to success than they believed. Resolve of the government was fading as a political transition took place. Banzer, due to illness (lung cancer), withdrew from public life, and power was increasingly passed to his vice president, who became president on 7 August 2001. This would be decisive for the Cocalero movement and for the country. Although Quiroga declared that he would continue Plan Dignity, he was not as strong-willed as Banzer. From the very beginning, he tried a softer approach towards the Cocaleros, which had immediate consequences.

In November, the Cocaleros upped the ante by declaring roadblocks between Santa Cruz and Cochabamba. The government declared that it would not allow the roads to be blocked and sent in 2000 police and Army reinforcements to secure natural chokepoints. Evo Morales declared a total blockade at Eterazama and concentrated a huge crowd of Cocaleros. This led to days of confrontation that reached a peak on 15 November, when clashes led to the deaths of three Cocaleros. Violence continued through 22 November, after which the government sought a way out by accepting the mediation of the Catholic Church, the Public Defender, and the Permanent Assembly on Human Rights from 26 to 28 November. The Cocaleros got exactly what they wanted. In exchange for lifting the roadblocks, the government agreed to suspend coca eradication in the Chapare.[186] Quiroga had lost his nerve in the face of increasingly large and violent political protests.

Quiroga's softer approach had immediate and palpable consequences. Coca crops quickly rose to 19,900 hectares by 1 June 2001. A GAO report noted that US and Bolivian officials attributed the rise to the Quiroga government's faltering commitment to crop elimination and a weakened governing coalition. They also indicated that they thought members of the government coalition might be making deals with the well-organized Cocaleros political party. In addition, critics, and even some who had supported Plan Dignity, claimed that while eradication has been successful in dramatically reducing coca cultivation, it had hurt the overall economy.[187]

The faltering of Quiroga's commitment to Plan Dignity and the weakening of the government coalition became the tipping point to include increasingly violent action against the government. Lenin's fusion of terrorism with the mass movement began to take place. After the Water War, armed squads that carried out violent action began to accompany virtually every protest.

---

[186] Lebedur, Ibid., 7.

[187] The General Accounting Office, Efforts to Develop Alternatives to Cultivating Illicit Crops in Colombia Have Made Little Progress and Face Serious Obstacles, 21.

Black February

The successes obtained from the Water War and the Highway Blockades encouraged others to carry out protests of their own, which in turn were magnified by the Cocaleros and their allies to support and strengthen their own position as a national power broker. This further weakened the government. In 2001 and 2002, violent social protests were daily occurrences, wearing down government will and ability to govern.[188] Increasing government incapacity in turn generated broader support for the 'political instrument' or Cocalero political party. The percentages of the vote in support of the MAS began to rise. President Gonzalo Sanchez de Lozada, or 'Goni', won a very close election in 2002, but perhaps as important, MAS achieved a very close second place. No party achieved a majority, so Goni became president of Bolivia with the support of less than a third of the population.

On 9 February 2003, the president announced a bill to freeze salaries and raise taxes by 12.5% for the top 20% of taxpayers.[189] This decision was made because of serious budget deficits and the desire to avoid the alternative of raising fuel prices, which would have a greater impact on the poor. The Cocaleros saw it as a measure that could be exploited given the relative weakness of Sanchez de Lozada's government. On 11 February, the Special Security Group Police in close proximity to the National Palace in La Paz went on strike to demand salary raises. On 12 February, the COB ceased negotiations with the government and declared a 24 hours period of civil disobedience. The CSUTCB also announced a 'rising' against the government. Finally, the Cocaleros, through the

---

[188] Camacho Balderrama, *La 'Rebelión' de Febrero*

[189] At this time, only 5% of Bolivians paid taxes

'People's High Command,' declared a strike in the city of Cocha-bamba.[190]

That same day, students from the Colegio Ayacucho, mobilized by the teachers' union, marched to Murillo Plaza and were confronted by soldiers of the Colorados Presidential Guard in riot gear, who attempted to stop them. The soldiers were forced to retreat into the Palace when rebel police fired tear gas at them, an eventuality for which they were unprepared, having no gas masks.[191] This left the outside of the building unprotected, and the students threw rocks, which they were carrying in their backpacks, at the government palace, breaking some of the windows.[192] The presidential guard then tossed tear gas grenades from inside the building down on the students and began launching gas grenades at the police on the other side of Murillo Plaza. The police launched tear gas grenades back at the army.

Attempts were made to mediate negotiations between the Army and Police, but these broke down. Eventually, the tear gas escalated to bullets, which according to the OAS were fired first by the police.[193] The Palace Guard was reinforced by elements of the Military Police, and additional police reinforced the strikers. Snipers on roofs, almost certainly from the Police Immediate Action Group or GA), began shooting into the palace.[194] This, combined with the possibility of a mob invasion of the palace, forced the President and his Ministers to evacuate via armored car.[195]

---

[190] Camacho Balderrama, op.cit.

[191] OAS General Secretariat, "Informe De La Organización De Los Estados Americanos Sobre Los Hechos De Febrero Del 2003 En Bolivia" May 2003, available at:
http://www.oas.org/OASpage/esp/Documentos/InfBO-051203.htm

[192] Ibid.

[193] Ibid.

[194] Ibid.

[195] Ibid.

By late afternoon and evening, there were no police patrolling the city. Organized mobs, some of which showed the same skills and tactical proficiency reported during the Water War and some led by police, set fire to the Vice Presidency, the Congressional Library and Archive, Ministry of Work and Sustainable Development, the Military Court, and the headquarters of the three political parties of the governing coalition.[196] Though students from the UMSA saved the Congressional Library and Archive from burning, preventing the loss of national historic documents, mobs with similar intent were mobilized in Oruro, Cochabamba, and Santa Cruz Clearly, an attempt was being made to destabilize the entire country.

On 13 February, clashes broke out between the military, deploying in various directions to restore order in La Paz and El Alto, and the mobs, resulting in approximately 11 killed and 50 wounded. Many claimed that the military reaction was excessive, and several officers were investigated and put on trial, although human rights groups claimed that the judicial process was slow and inefficient.[197] At the request of the Bolivian government, a multinational team from the OAS came to Bolivia to investigate and found that the army had acted legitimately and proportionately, although it questioned some of the rules of engagement and decisions made by specific officers. In general, the OAS laid responsibility for the violence squarely on the police.[198] Ominously, the reports of organized groups operating during the events again went largely unexamined.

---

[196] OAS General Secretariat, op.cit.

[197] Amnesty International, "Bolivia, Crisis y Justicia". November 30, 2004, available: https://www.amnesty.org/es/documents/amr18/006/2004/es/

[198] OAS General Secretariat, op.cit.

Gas War (Black October)

Black February showed the Cocaleros that their thesis of action against the political center was correct. In addition, the relative weakness of the national government made it so that a relatively small political conflict could be escalated through mass protests, and peripheral violence into a major national crisis that could push the government to the edge of collapse. The Cocaleros were certain that if they pushed just a little harder, the 'next time' would drive the government across the point of no return. It was now merely a matter of time before the next major event which they determined would be the culminating event.

The Cocaleros began to prepare by organizing several groups: the CSUTCB, which controlled the Aymara-dominated high plain around La Paz; the Central Obrera Regional or COR, which controlled the gateway to La Paz, El Alto; and the Unión Revolucionaria de Maestros (URMA), which controlled La Paz itself. Each received money and various other forms of support, and agreements were made to mobilize forces, when the time was right. Felipe Quispe, leader of the CSUTCB, later revealed that a plan was developed to take place in three phases, with Venezuela and various NGOs providing funding.[199] The phases, at least for CSUTCB, were: Phase Flea, provoke the enemy and bite him; *Phase Fire Ant* (Sikititl), swarm the enemy with protests; and Phase Taraxchi, the final assault on the establishments and homes of the powerful and oligarchy.[200] These phases correspond quite well to Lenin's concepts of escalation from protest to armed uprising. While this concept may have been unique to the CSUTCB,

---

[199] Ibid.

[200] René Quenallata, "El Mallku revela que falló una emboscada para matar a Sánchez Berzaín". EJU!, April 8, 2013. Available at: https://eju.tv/2013/08/el-mallku-revela-que-fall-una-emboscada-para-matar-a-snchez-berzan/

the overall plan was similar to that animating all of the major opponents of the state. The opportunity to implement the plan presented itself in September and October of that same year, a series of events that is commonly called 'The Gas War' or 'Black October.'

The government was experiencing serious trouble with the national budget. The solution seemed to be natural gas. To earn additional revenue, the Bolivian government was exploring deals to sell part of its huge reserves to American and Mexican firms. The Sanchez de Lozada government estimated that sales to Mexico alone were projected to produce government revenues of USD 400 million per year over a period of 20 years. The opposition claimed that this deal only benefited the multi-national companies involved.

Still, it was the decision to build a pipeline from Bolivia to export the gas north via the port of Mejillones, Chile that led to explosion. The plan was for the gas to be sent via pipeline to Chile, where it would be liquefied and then exported. In Bolivia, wounded national pride over the loss of its coast to Chile in the War of the Pacific, 1879-1883, had left sensitivity to any such dealings with Chile. Popular opinion favored instead a pipeline to the Port of 110, Peru. This meant a pipeline that was 161 miles longer than the proposed pipeline to Mejillones, thus much more expensive, making it economically less attractive. However, the Peruvians tried to make the option attractive by offering very generous terms to the Bolivians. The opposition also wanted to keep more of the money in the country by doing the liquefaction processing in Bolivia. President Quiroga had declined to make a decision and left it to Sanchez de Losada when he became president in 2002. Sanchez de Losada, who was a pragmatist, expressed a preference for the Chile route. The Cocaleros and their allies took full advantage of this preference.

CSUTCB made the opening move to implement Phase Flea. The first clash took place at Warisata, a major Aymara center on the road to Lake Titicaca, where the locals blocked the highways during the night to protest — not the sale of gas via Chile — rather the government's failure to comply with an agreement signed earlier by government ministers. The blockades trapped many international tourists. The military was sent on 20 September to rescue the tourists and to sort out the situation. As they began making arrests and breaking up the crowds, the protesters called CSUTCB head Felipe Quispe concerning the arrests of three protest leaders and claimed that the army was going to kill them. Quispe ordered those of his followers who were members of the EGTK,[201] or who had been trained in guerrilla warfare, to dig up the weapons and ambush the security forces.[202] The ambush killed one policeman and wounded several others.[203] The objective of the ambush was to attract response and assassinate Minister of Defense Carlos Sánchez Berzafn, but he left Warisata in a helicopter, which CSUTCB had not anticipated.[204] The army reported they were attacked with modern, high caliber weapons. The protesters claimed that they were only using old Chaco War weapons that had been distributed to the popular militias in the 1950s.[205] In the subsequent firefight, four locals were killed, including an 8-year old girl, and the military was able to break the blockade.

Phase Flea was a total success. The death of the girl helped distract the nation from the reality that CSUTCB had initiated the violence; it stirred emotions and served as an initial rallying cry for a much larger protest against the government. The successful

---

[201] Ejército Guerrillero Tupak Katari, a relatively obscure guerrilla group.

[202] Guisela López, "Yo ordené la emboscada de Warisata." *Semanario Pulso*, May 28, 2006.

[203] "Fuego cruzado en Warisata deja 5 muertos y heridos", Bolivia, September 21, 2003. Available at:
https://www.bolivia.com/noticias/AutoNoticias/DetalleNoticia16029.asp

[204] René Quenallata, op. cit.

[205] Guisela López, "Warisata: la masacre de hace un año todavía duele". *El Deber,* September 2004

mobilization of mass protests put into motion Phase Fire Ant. As Felipe Quispe admitted years later, cadre were sent to whip up the masses.[206]

On 25 September, the COB (essentially, the miners' federation) declared it was joining the protests; on 26 September, Evo Morales' MAS joined; and on 27 September, CSUTCB joined. On 29 September, an 'indefinite' strike was declared. Members of the three organizations began converging on La Paz on 3 October.

The Cocaleros anticipated that this next phase would see the definitive merger of 'terrorism with the mass movement,' in other words, that it would get very violent, that the government might lash out aggressively out of desperation and target their leaders. To ensure the survival of their leaders and make sure that the Cocaleros would be in a position to pick up the pieces after it was over, Evo Morales was sent out of the country. He travelled to Libya, Geneva, and Caracas and only returned when the danger had passed, and the outcome of the uprising was relatively assured.[207]

The key to the protest was the city of El Alto, the gateway to the city of La Paz. La Paz is built in a bowl-like valley surrounded on all sides by steep slopes. At the top is the Altiplano or high plains. La Paz is connected to eastern Bolivia by a highway that winds up the steep slopes and comes out on this high plain. Most commodities (food, fuel, and other items) that supply La Paz pass along this road from eastern Bolivia. Over the years, mostly poor people occupied the area in the Altiplano along the road on the edge of the slopes leading down into La Paz. This area was incorporated

---

[206] René Quenallata, op.cit.

[207] "Felipe Quispe: Evo Morales huyó a Libia en octubre negro de 2003", *El Diario*, March 8, 2018. Available at:
https://www.eldiario.net/noticias/2018/2018_03/nt180308/polit-ica.php?n=89&-evo-morales-huyo-a-libia-en-octubre-negro-de-2003

into a city known as El Alto.[208] The international airport is also nearby, so whoever controls El Alto controls land and air access to La Paz. Knowing this, the insurgents gathered their forces here on October 8 and blocked the roads. They especially focused on cutting off fuel supplies into the city.

Between 9 and 12 October, there were serious clashes between armed and semi-armed marchers, particularly miners from Oruro, and government security forces. While most of the marchers were unarmed, accompanying the marches were groups of young men with weapons and explosives. Among them were members of EGTK, but it was later reported that documents from the Raul Reyes computers captured in Ecuador revealed that among the armed squads were up to 60 members of the Colombian FARC.[209] In this way, the marches were accompanied by selective acts of violence and sabotage. Among the most notable acts: on 10 October, a natural gas pipeline into La Paz was dynamited near the 'Boliviana' Beer plant; on 13 October, three overhead crosswalks were dynamited along the road to Río Seco; and on 15 October, a train on the El Alto to La Paz track was derailed in such a manner as to block the highway between El Alto and La Paz. In addition, numerous commercial locales were looted and burned, some by the armed squads and some by the unarmed masses.

The clashes grew in violence. On the 9th, two people were killed and 26 wounded in the clashes. Stopped tanker trucks began to pile up behind government lines. On 10 October, the government flew in reinforcements from other parts of the country. On the 11th, three more people were killed, and dozens wounded in an attempt to break the blockade and send two tanker trucks into La Paz. This effort was not successful, and attempts to mediate failed because

---

[208] 'The Heights' in English.

[209] "Un abogado dice que las FARC actuaron el 2003", *Eju!,* October 17, 2019. Available:
http://eju.tv/2008/10/un-abogado-dice-que-las-farc-actuaron-el-2003/

the leaders of the protests were not interested in negotiating, Their objective was to overthrow President Sanchez de Lozada.

The most violent day was 12 October, when the military was ordered to force the blockades with 12 tanker trucks, six for civilian consumption and six for the military. Resistance was fierce, and the opposition claimed that 26 people were killed and more than 100 wounded in the clashes.[210] The violence did not consist of the army and police firing indiscriminately at unarmed civilians as has often been portrayed. There was give and take, with the armed squads among the protesters producing losses among the security forces, and the security forces firing back. On 14 October, the Association of Parents reported that approximately 17 soldiers had been killed in the clashes. These losses were not reported by the government.[211] This was clear evidence that the violence was not one way.

On 13 October, several additional organizations joined the marchers: The National Confederation of Transporters, the Confederation of Rural Teachers, the Confederation of Urban Education Workers of Bolivia, the Departmental Federation of Urban Workers of La Paz, and the Confederation of Health Workers. In addition, Cocaleros in the Chapare set up roadblocks to support the roadblocks in El Alto. Realizing they could no longer hold out against this mob unless they wanted to commit a massacre, the army abandoned El Alto and withdrew into La Paz proper during the night.

On 14 and 15 October, there was a lull, which both sides used to reorganize and gather forces. The only violence was a clash between the army and a column of miners from Oruro making their way down into to La Paz. Three died. Meanwhile, the three parties of the government coalition met and came up with a compromise

---

[210] http://www.rebelion.org/homeroteca/bolivia/O31018po.htm

[211] http://www.rebelion.org/homeroteca/bolivia/O31018po.htm

proposal on natural gas. This went nowhere, as that had never been the actual issue in play. The real objective had always been the overthrow of the government. Claiming that they couldn't compromise because now there was blood on the government's hands, Evo Morales and Felipe Quispe ordered a full advance into La Paz.

Insurgent victory

On 16 October, 100,000 marchers descended into La Paz and surrounded the government buildings. They threatened to employ 'total violence' if the government did not resign. The Cocaleros were willing to take the confrontation to the next level, open civil war. The government and establishment politicians were not. They still thought they could make deals. As a result, on 1 7 October, Gonzalo Sanchez de Lozada and his cabinet resigned as the government administration of Bolivia, a capitulation that led the Cocaleros to order as unnecessary the third phase, Taraxchi.

Though some, such as Felipe Quispe, one of the more radical leaders, wanted to implement Phase 3 and bring the revolution to a quick and bloody end, the Cocaleros were more pragmatic. To them, Phase 3 was only to be implemented in case there was no other alternative. Otherwise, it was not a good optic *vis-à-vis* the international community. If the whole government resigned, it would be obvious that the constitutional order had been broken and that power had been seized through insurrection. MAS wanted power, but it wanted the appearance of winning through at least a modicum of institutional legitimacy. It knew that this was important to the outside world and understood the power of perception.

The Cocalero trump card was Vice President Carlos Mesa. Before becoming the Vice President, he had been a journalist and was perceived by Sanchez de Lozada's advisors to be the right complement to enable Sanchez to win the 2002 elections, because his popularity and influence on public opinion were seen as a boost to the business-like, blunt personality of Goni. The problem was that Mesa was not ideologically tied to Sanchez de Lozada or his party. To convince him to accept the nomination to Vice President, he was bribed. This fact did not escape the Cocaleros' intelligence, which was very efficient in gathering this type of data on all kinds of political personalities across the spectrum of Bolivian politics. During the February 2003 crisis, Mesa had threatened resignation and only desisted when he asked for and received another substantial sum to retain his loyalty. The Cocaleros knew this and therefore saw him as someone who could be manipulated for the right price.

Evo Morales, who had purposefully avoided most of the action, now suddenly appeared, swiftly approaching Vice-President Carlos Mesa to offer him both power and money to stay in place and create the illusion that, although there had been a popular uprising, the constitutional order had been maintained. The only thing that had happened had been the resignation of a 'criminal' and unpopular president. Mesa agreed and withdrew his initial resignation. He would serve as president for the nearly two following years.[212]

It was a Cocalero masterstroke. Mesa was asked for and delivered an executive order that in its essence characterized the insurgents as innocent protesters and therefore not legally responsible for any of the violence, while at the same time putting all of the responsibility on the overthrown president, his cabinet (except for Mesa), and the military high command. They were to all be captured and tried for their 'crimes.'

Morales' verbal agreement with Mesa also stipulated that the latter would only serve as a caretaker president and focus on preparing for new elections and a new government, which if they occurred soon, while the Cocaleros still had the initiative, would be handily

---

[212] "Un abogado dice que las FARC actuaron el 2003", Eju!, October 17, 2019. Available:
http://eju.tv/2008/10/un-abogado-dice-que-las-farc-actuaron-el-2003/

won by Evo Morales. At first Mesa stuck to his deal and began to take steps to prepare the way for the next government. He called for a referendum on the gas industry as well as for a convention to write a new constitution. These measures were approved. This was legally convenient to justify the MAS plan to radically alter Bolivian government and society. Also, in this way, rather than provoking opposition by coming up with the measures themselves, they would be able to claim that they were merely fulfilling the mandate of the previous government. This again follows Lenin's strategy closely. He called for the creation of a provisional government, amnesty for all the 'fighters,' and a constituent assembly to consolidate the legitimacy of the victory won by the mass uprising.[213]

Mesa pushed for nationalization of Bolivia's gas industry. A law was passed to increase taxes from 27 to 50% on exported gas. On the international front, he pushed for sovereign access through Chile of a Pacific Ocean port. His government also modified the existing constitution to allow for the convening of a constituent assembly. The assembly was approved but did not take place under Carlos Mesa, instead during Evo Morales' first term. In this way, it was portrayed as merely the continuation of the constitutional mandate.

In general, the political climate was calmer during the first 18 months of the Mesa government, because Mesa kept most of his promises to Morales. This allowed Bolivia to increase its exports and implement an austerity plan that greatly reduced the debt. However, Mesa's success caused him to develop ambitions of staying in power until 2007, the end of Sanchez de Lozada's constitutional term. Mesa's mistake was to believe that the Cocaleros would allow him to fulfill the constitutional mandate. Their reason for refusing to go along with this move was simple: If Mesa continued to enjoy success and stayed in place until 2007, there was

---

[213] See Note 22.

nothing that guaranteed that the Cocalero coalition with the other social movement organizations would be able to maintain cohesion and win the subsequent elections. For the moment, they had cohesion and the initiative, and wanted to take advantage of it.

The Cocaleros were not going to allow Mesa to break the verbal agreement with Morales. To make matters worse for Mesa, since he did not belong to a political party, he began to face resistance from the traditional parties as well, who had ambitions of their own. None had ever regarded him as anything but a temporary caretaker. The latter undermined him in Congress, for example, approving a hydrocarbons law that did not call for total nationalization. Since the Gas War rallying banner had been gas nationalization, the Cocaleros used the new hydrocarbons law as a pretext to force Mesa out of power as they had Goni. They began new marches, again blocking the roads and highways across the country in Cochabamba, La Paz, Sucre, Santa Cruz, Montero, Potosi, and Oruro.

Caught between these marches and opposition in Congress, Mesa continuing in power became impossible. After several months of the chaos, he submitted his resignation on March 6, 2005. Congress did not accept it, but the act marked the end of any cooperation between Mesa and Congress, which began to resist all of his initiatives, forcing him to rule by decree. Facing mounting opposition from both the right and the left, he successfully resigned on June 6, 2005.[214]

Congress's plan was to make the President of the Senate, Hormando Vaca Diez (MIR), the new President of Bolivia, or if he wouldn't or couldn't, to turn to the President of Congress, Mario Cossío (MNR)t to finish Goni's constitutional presidential term. The Cocaleros and their allies were filling La Paz with protesters

---

[214] Alex Contreras Baspineiro, "¡Qué se vayan todos! Renunció el presidente Mesa, los problemas suman y siguen", June 7, 2005. Available at: https://www.alainet.org/es/active/8383

to prevent this from happening. Thinking they could out-maneuver the Cocaleros by moving the meeting, it was decided to hold the legislative session in Sucre, Bolivia's historical capital. This was a mistake because Sucre is only accessible by two roads, which are easily blocked, and an airport with a precarious schedule due to weather conditions. Upon learning that the Legislature was moving to Sucre, the Cocalero-led opposition immediately began assembling marchers to besiege that city. They moved much quicker than the Legislature had anticipated, demonstrating their capacity to organize and coordinate their masses. The legislators moved by air, and the military put on a display of force to keep the protesters out of the urban area; but it was Bolivia's winter, and weather prevented all of the legislators from arriving quickly. This meant that they could not do a quick vote and present the country with a fait accompli. Armed elements accompanied the marchers and were in place before the Legislature could act. They sent a warning to the Legislature that if Hormando Vaca Diez or Mario Cossío were made president, there would be civil war.[215]

Although their main tactic was not military action, they were prepared to use it on a massive scale. The Cocaleros demanded that the President of the Supreme Court, Eduardo Rodríguez Veltzé, become president with the sole mandate to prepare new presidential elections.[216] Besieged and threa[217]tened in Sucre, and unwilling to go to war, the Legislature caved in to the Cocaleros' demands. The elections were held in December 2005 and resulted in a clear victory for Evo Morales and MAS. The insurgency was now consolidated, and the uprising legitimized through internationally recognized elections.

---

[215] Ibid.

[216] Ibid.

[217] See Tomas Marks, "Terrorism as Method in Nepali Maoist Insurgency, 1996-2016," *Smalls Wars & Insurgencies,* 81-118, Feb 17, 2017

Conclusions

Reflecting on the success of the Bolivian insurgency, it is evident that the Cocaleros won because they applied the correct combination of all forms of struggle. Leading the forms of struggle were semi-violent protests versus open military conflict. This is remarkable given the almost exclusive tradition in Latin America of insurgency via mostly armed conflict, but is not unlike what has recently been attempted elsewhere. The Cocaleros correctly assessed the relative correlation of forces and applied that combination of forms of struggle which carried them to victory. The most important characteristic that led the Cocaleros to this correct combination was their eminent pragmatism, over ideological dogmatism, yet profound understanding of insurgency and revolutionary theory. The outcome was a brilliant strategic victory, so much so that the victory was not really perceived by the international public as an insurgency.

What is clear is that the strategy was not necessarily brilliant from its conception but rather became so as it adapted and evolved. First in importance was its evolution in its understanding of power. Initially, it was merely the power to stop eradication at the local level. This did not work, so the Cocaleros sought to influence policy through a co-opted political party. This did not work very well, either, so they sought to create their own political party to share political power; and while this gave them significant influence, it did not give them control. Thus, they decided to take power to institute a new order to their liking and design.

The political instrument (as they called their party) was vital, because it allowed them to consolidate power and suborn like-minded fellow travelers even as the real battle for power was fought in the streets. There were two approaches. The first, drawn from great experience in the mines, was that of the experienced union leaders and organizers who were familiar with the power

189

that had been achieved by the miners through their mass protests since the 1952 revolution. The second was drawn from the *ferreros* or the believers in guns, who understood that as necessary power would not be obtained without major violence if not civil war.

Fortunately for the Cocaleros, the former dominated, because there was a tradition of mass protests and a history of limited successes obtained. The state may have surrendered but averted major tragedy. Nevertheless, the second approach was a significant element, employed to protect the Cocaleros' income and mass actions, as well as being held in reserve in case the Cocaleros really ran into a brick wall and needed extraordinary violence to blast open the way. Perhaps Bolivia would have turned into a typical guerrilla warfare insurgency had President Banzer lived to complete his second term and Plan Dignity been seen through to the end. However, this did not happen, and the Qurioga government did not have the stomach to confront the Cocaleros at the level to which they were willing to take matters.

Due to this, the second brilliant aspect of the Cocalero insurgent strategy was their limited, targeted application of violence, with the Leninist understanding that it had to be subordinate to the political struggle and only selectively employed. First, it was used to protect drug trafficking, the source of Cocalero money. In this, the insurgency was able to avoid detection by attributing the violence to faceless 'drug traffickers.' Additionally, at critical moments, the Cocaleros did resort to violence that produced significant casualties and brought the country to the brink of open war. This demonstrated that they had the will and the means to go to the next level. The government always blinked at these moments, which slowly but systematically tipped the balance of power in the Cocaleros' favor. This tipping process became increasingly visible after 2000. The big moments were the Water War, the November 2001 marches in the Chapare, Black February, the Gas War, the marches to overthrow Mesa, and the siege of Sucre. The scale of violence or willingness to employ violence escalated with each event but never reached open warfare, even though the situation often went right to the brink of open warfare. Each time, the government shied from the fight. Thus, each incident of brinkmanship squeezed a significant political concession from the state and paved the way for an eventual Morales political victory. The Cocaleros applied violence just enough to make systematic progress towards their ultimate objective, to take power, but not enough violence to reveal the insurgency and/or provoke a strong reaction, either from the government or its international backers.

This clearly demonstrates a return to a more Leninist approach to insurgency in Latin America from the recently dominant Maoist trend of using violence as the principle form of struggle. Such emphasis, practitioners in other struggles might note (e.g. Nepal or the Philippines), could not only be assessed as doctrinally flawed (ignoring e.g. the prescription by Mao that the united front was the decisive element) but in many ways as culturally specific to the region. Not in question, though, is that changing Latin American conditions have caused a reconsideration of insurgent strategy, most particularly, in the Bolivia case. The reality was that a weak, poor democracy suffering significant levels of corruption simply lacked the ability to muster sufficient legitimacy and hence coercive power.

The high political cost of the use of military force — due to alleged and real human rights abuses during the Cold War — and significantly reduced military budgets after 1990, with corresponding reductions of military capabilities, left a vacuum in both self-defense and coercive capacities much less capabilities. The police had neither the will nor the ability to fill the resulting vacuum. This was exacerbated by the perception that in democracy, societies needed less policing, leading to the design of deliberately weaker forces that were unequal to the security challenge. Subsequent experience showed that for the democratic age, perhaps greater, more capable policing was required to provide adequate security in post-Cold War Latin America.

Perhaps as importantly, post-Cold War judicial systems have remained weak and politicized in Latin America, and levels of impunity are relatively high. In this sense, in the post-Cold War era, far more avenues for struggle are open to radical opposition political groups, making it unnecessary to rely so heavily on violence, even as the very weakness of the state compels the use of some level of violence as both an attractive and effective option.

Finally, the Cocaleros understood that the motor of the insurgency was money. Money was more important than guns. Money sustained the organization, gave it coherence and power. Money paid for the armed organization that defended the Coca. Money paid for the marchers and sustained them over prolonged periods of time, helping them to outlast the patience of the government. Money paid for the political instrument and helped it grow quickly into the second force of the country. Money bought non-Cocalero social organizations and bent them to the Cocaleros' will. Money corrupted government officials and prevented the efficient application of counter-narcotics and security strategies. Money was available in previously undreamed of quantities through illicit markets. This is perhaps one of the most significant differences between Cold War and Post-Cold War insurgencies in Latin America and around the globe.

As we look to the near future, we can expect that similar insurgent strategies will be applied against governments where similar conditions exist. Colombia, for example, is a country to watch. Is FARC really negotiating the demobilization of its forces and the reincorporation of its members into Colombian society as M-19 did or the FMLN did in El Salvador? Or, is it using the peace process to transform its struggle to look something like Bolivia?[218]

---

[218] Refer to contributions by Ospina and Marks in this special issue.

FARC is in a much different situation than were FMLN or M-19. It has a great deal of money compared to previous insurgencies. Why would it suddenly give it up to become an unpopular, weak political party? Most of the governments of the countries in the region are currently sympathetic to FARC's political cause, and FARC has been increasingly mobilizing large country-wide marches to express opposition to the government. Ten years ago, these marches hardly existed. Now, they are a regular feature of the Colombian political landscape, mobilizing 10,000, 30,000, or even 60,000 marchers. Colombia appears to be a much stronger democracy than Bolivia ever was, but it still has many of the same problems that Bolivia did. There is considerable drug trafficking in Colombia. Certain regions of Colombia still lack substantial security, and corruption is still a significant problem, even if much reduced from thirty years ago. Thus, it remains to be seen what is at hand. Regardless, the emergence of a new model of insurgency, one still built upon the popular mobilization of people's war but more attuned to new global realities, is a reality.

General References

Amnesty International. "Bolivia, Crisis y Justicia: Jornadas de violencia en febrero y octubre del 2003", November 30, 2004.

BARRERO CORDERO, Juan. "La Guerra del Agua en Cochabamba: un caso de palabras que hablan mal." *Investigación Ambiental Ciencia y Política Pública*, No. 1 (2009):91-100.

BERRY, LaVerle et al. "A global overview of narcotics-funded terrorist and other extremist groups". A report prepared by the Federal Research Division, Library of Congress under an Interagency Agreement with the Department of Defense, May 2002.

BLANCO, Juan Antonio; Cartaya Rolando; Dominguez, Luis; and Ocando, Casto. *Cubazuela: Chronicle of a Cuban Intervention* Miami: Foundation for Human Rights in Cuba, 2019.

BREWER, Jacqueline. *Convergence: Illicit Networks and National Security in the Age of Globalization.* Washington, DC: National Defense University Press, 2013.

CAMACHO BALDERRAMA, Natalia. "La Rebelión de Febrero: una Historia que no se puede reeditar." Buenos Aires: Biblioteca Clacso, 2003.

Center por Study of Democracy. "Examining the Links between Organized Crime and Corruption", 2010.

CHRISTINO, Marcio Sergio; TOGNOLLI, Claudio. *Laços de sangue: a história secreta do PCC*. São Paulo: Matrix Editora, 2017.

CICAD. "Evaluación del Plan Dignidad". Washington, DC: Organización de Estados Americanos, n.d.

CONTRERAS BASPINEIRO, Alex. "Qué se vayan todos! Renunció el presidente Mesa, los problemas suman y siguen." *ALAINET*, June 7, 2005.

CORSON, William R. and Crowley, Robert T. The New KGB: Engine of Soviet Power, New York: Morrow, 1985

COUTINHO, "Leonardo. Cai a fronteira entre o regime venezuelano e o narcotráfico." *Veja*, 13 November2015.

COUTINHO, Leonardo. "Iran and Hezbollah in the Western Hemisphere: statement before the US House of Representatives Committee on Foreign Affairs Subcommittee on the Western Hemisphere & Subcommittee on the Middle East and North Africa". Washington (DC), Serial number 114-34, 03/18/2015a. p. 76-81.

COUTINHO, Leonardo. "Os gigolôs da paz." *Veja*, 31 January 2018.

COUTINHO, Leonardo. "Turning the tables: how Brazil defeated an ISIS threat." *Global Dispatch*, Center for a Secure Free Society, Washington, D.C., issue 5, September 2017.

COUTINHO, Leonardo. *Hugo Chávez, o espectro: como o presidente venezuelano alimentou o narcotráfico, financiou o terrorismo e promoveu a desordem global*. Belo Horizonte: Vestígio, 2018.

"CPI acusa PC de formar quadrilha". *Jornal do Brasil*, Rio de Janeiro, ano CII, n. 109, 26 June 1992.

DAROCA OLLERT, Santiago. "Protesta y Acción Social en Cochabamba." *Los Cuadernos de Trabajo*, Programa de Naciones Unidas para el Desarrollo, (n.d.).

Defensor del Pueblo. "Estudio de Violencia Intrafamiliar en Contextos de Violencia Generalizada." Trópico Cochabambino. n.p., 2006.

DEPARTMENT OF JUSTICE. Office of Public Affairs. Manssor Arbabsiar Sentenced in New York City Federal Court to 25 Years in Prison for Conspiring with Iranian Military Officials to Assassinate the Saudi Arabian Ambassador to the United States. May 30, 2013.

DOUGLASS, Joseph. *Red Cocaine: The Drugging of America and the West.* Edward Harle Limited, 1999

"Drugs, Russia And Terrorism, Part 1". Newsmax, March 7, 2002

EHRENFELD, Rachel, *Narco-Terrorism and the Cuban Connection,* Washington, DC: The Cuban American National Foundation, 1988

EMBARGOS de Declaração na Extradição 936 – República Italiana. In: *Revista Trimestral de Jurisprudência*, Supremo Tribunal Federal, v. 196, n. 3, p. 744-751, abr./jun. 2006

FARAH, Douglas *Bolivia: Silent partner in the Bolivarian joint criminal enterprise: Evo Morales, the MAS and Regional Instability.* Miami: Interamerican Institute of Democracy, 2019

FARAH, Douglas. "A Strategic Overview of Latin America Identifying New Convergence Centers, Forgotten Territories, and Vital Hubs for Transnational Organized Crime". *Strategic Perspectives* #28, Institute for National Strategic Studies; January 2009.

FARAH, Douglas. *Cuba's role in the Bolivarian radical populist movement's dismantling democracy.* Miami: Interamerican Institute of Democracy, 2018

Federation of American Scientists. "Consequences for US Strategic Interests" in *International Crime Threat Assessment.* December 2000.
https://fas.org/irp/threat/pub45270chap4.html

FLYNN, Michael. *The Field of Fight: How We Can Win the Global War Against Radical Islam and Its Allies*. New York: St. Martin's Press, 2016

FÓRUM BRASILEIRO DE SEGURANÇA PÚBLICA. *Anuário Brasileiro de Segurança Pública 2018*. Segurança Pública em números.

FUENTES, Norberto. *Narcotráfico y tareas revolucionarias. El concepto cubano.* Miami: Ediciones Universal, 2002

Government of the Republic of Bolivia. "Memoria: Gobierno Constitucional Hugo Banzer Suarez 1997-2001" La Paz: Imprenta Oficial, 2002.

HARTMAN, Bob *Inside DEA Operation Snowcap*. United State: Trafford Publishing, 2011

HUMIRE, Joseph M. *Argentina: Latin America's New Leader in Counterterrorism*, Gatestone Institute, July 2019

International Campaign to Ban Landmines. "Landmine Monitoring Report 2004."

ISIS, *How to Survive in the West: A Mujahid Guide*, 2015

KEEFE, Patrick Radden. "The trafficker: the decades-long battles to catch an international arms broker". *The New Yorker*, February 8, 2010.

KUHN, T.S. *The Structure of Scientific Revolutions*. Chicago, IL: University of Chicago Press, 1962

LEALI, Francisco. "Polícia federal aponta elo entre facção brasileira e Hezbollah." *O Globo*, 9 November 2014.

LEDEBUR, Kathryn. "Coca y Conflicto en el Chapare". Washington, DC: Washington Office on Latin America (WOLA), July 2002.

LENIN, Vladimir I. "The Third Congress of the R.S.D.L.P. April 25—May 10, 1905." Draft Resolution of the Armed Uprising.

LENIN, Vladimir I. "A Militant Agreement for the Uprising." 1905.

LENIN, Vladimir I. "Guerrilla Warfare." 1906.

LENIN, Vladimir I. "Lessons of the Moscow Uprising." 1906.

LEVITT, Matthew. "Hizbullah narco-terrorism: a growing cross-border threat." IHS Defence, Risk and Security Consulting, Washington, D.C.,2012.

LEVY, Aida. *El rey de cocaína: Mi vida con Roberto Suárez Gómez y el nacimiento del primer narcoestado.* Mexico D.F.: Random House, 2013

LIANG, Qiao e XIANGSUI, Wang. *Unrestricted Warfare.* Beijing. PLA Literature and Arts Publishing House. February 1999.

LÓPEZ, Guisela. "Hay 100 desactivadores de cazabobos." *El Deber*, March 15, 2004.

LÓPEZ, Guisela. "Warisata: la masacre de hace un año todavía duele." *El Deber*, September 20, 2004.

LÓPEZ, Guisela. "Yo ordené la emboscada de Warisata." *Semanario Pulso,* May 28, 2006.

LUCCHELLI, Giuseppe. "Il Vero Killer? Detenuto in un Altro-Paese." *La Repubblica*, Roma, 02/09/1992.

MAGYAR, Bálint, *The Post- Communist Mafia State. The Case of Hungary*, Hungary, 2016

MARKS, Thomas & Rich, Paul. "Back to the future – people's war in the 21st century". *Small Wars & Insurgencies*. Vol. 28, No. 3 (2017).

MARKS, Thomas A. "Terrorism as Method in Nepali Maoist Insurgency, 1996-2016." *Small wars and Insurgencies* Vol. 28, No. 1 (2017).

MARKS, Thomas A. *Counterrevolution in China: Wang Sheng and the Kuomingtang*. London: Frank Cass, 1998.

MARKS, Thomas A. *Maoist People's War in Post-Vietnam Asia*. Bangkok: White Lotus, 2007.

MCCAULEY, Kevin N. *Russian Influence Campaigns against the West: From the Cold War to Putin*. North Charleston: CreateSpace. 2016

MENDELL, William W. "Counterdrug Strategy - Illusive Victory: From Blast Furnace to Green Sweep". *Military Review,* December 1992:74-87.

MEYER, Josh. *The Secret Backstory of How Obama let Hezbollah off the Hook*. *Politico*, 2017

MITCHELL, Matthew. *Not Your Father's Coast Guard: The Untold Story of U.S. Coast Guard Special Forces*. Bloomington: Author House. 2009

NAÍM, Moisés, "Mafia States. Organized Crime Takes Office". *Foreign Affairs*, May/June 2012

NAVIA GABRIEL, Roberto, and Pinto Cascán, Darwin. "Mutilados y olvidados de Chapare". *El Deber*, August 5, 2007.

NHU TANG, Truong. A Vietcong Memoir: An inside Account of the Vietnam War and Its Aftermath, New York: Vintage Books, 1986.

"Nuevas denuncias para el gobierno de Chávez. El poder judicial venezolano está penetrado por el narcotráfico". *El Imparcial*, América, May 10, 2012.

Organization of American States. "Informe de La Organización de Los Estados Americanos (OEA) sobre los Hechos de Febrero del 2003 en Bolivia."

OTTOLENGHI, Emanuele. "Examining the effectiveness of Kingpin Designation Act in the Western Hemisphere." Foundation for Defense of Democracies, November 8, 2017.

PACEPA, Ion Mihai & Rychlak, Ronald. *Disinformation: Former Spy Chief Reveals Secret Strategies for Undermining Freedom, Attacking Religion, and Promoting Terrorism.* WND Books, 2013

PIKE, Douglas. *PAVN: People's Army of Vietnam.* Novato, CA: Presidio Press, 1986.

PRESÍDIO FEDERAL DE MS recebe suspeitos de integrar Hezbollah. G1, 24 enero 2008

PURVIS, Stephen, *Close But No Cigar. A True Story of Prison Life in Castro's Cuba*, London: Weidenfeld & Nicolson, 2018

QUISPE HUANCA, Felipe. "Bolivia Recuerda los Hechos de Febrero Negro." February 2013. Accessed October 3, 2014. boliviaprensa.com

QUISPE HUANCA, Felipe. "CSUTCB, máxima instancia superior de las rebeliones." bolpress.com, July 4, 2014.

QUISPE HUANCA, Felipe. "El Mallku revela que falló una emboscada para matar a Sánchez Berzaín." August 4, 2013. EJu.tv

QUISPE HUANCA, Felipe. "Evo Morales escapó a Libia en hechos de octubre de 2003." November 10, 2010. Fmbolivia.com.bo

QUISPE HUANCA, Felipe. "Fuego cruzado en Warisata deja 5 muertos y heridos." September 21, 2003. www.bolivia.com

QUISPE HUANCA, Felipe. "Un abogado dice que las FARC actuaron el 2003." Eju.tv. October 17, 2008.

QUISPE HUANCA, Felipe. "Yo Ordené la Emboscada de Warisata." May 28, 2006. www.comocayogoni.com

RAFAEL, Tony. *The Mexican Mafia*. Encounter Books, 2007

RAPOPORT, David C. *The Four Waves of Modern Terror: International Dimensions and Consequences*. Geneva: UCLA, 2011.

RAVINES, Eudocio, *La Gran Estafa* Mexico: Libros y Revistas S.A, 1952

RODRIGUEZ, Alberto K. "Evitar la Confrontación: Entrevista con Filemón Escobar." *Encuentro* No. 44. July 20, 2007.

SÁNCHEZ BERZAÍN, Carlos. *Castrochavismo: Crimen Organizado en Las Américas*. Miami: Interamerican Institute for Democracy, 2019

SAPORI, Luís Flávio; SOARES, Gláucio Ary Dillon. *Por que cresce a violência no Brasil?* Belo Horizonte: Autêntica Editora/Editora PUC Minas, 2014.

SHULTZ, Jim, and Melissa Crane Draper, eds. *Desafiando la Globalización: Historias de la Experiencia Boliviano*. La Paz: Plural Editores, 2008.

SNEGOVAYA, Maria, "The Implications of Russia's Mafia State". *American Interest*. December 23rd, 2015

STORRS, Larry K. "Andean Regional Initiative (ARI): FY2002 Supplemental and FY2003 Assistance for Colombia and Neighbors". Washington, DC: Congressional Research Service, June 12, 2002.

TALEB, Nassim Nicholas. *The Black Swan: The impact the highly improbable.* New York: Random House, 2007.

The General Accounting Office. "Efforts to Develop Alternatives to Cultivating Illicit Crops in Colombia Have Made Little Progress and Face Serious Obstacles." GAO-02-291 February 2002, 21.

U.S. Department of Justice. "Overview of the Law Enforcement Strategy to Combat International Organized Crime." Special Report, April 2008

U.S. Department of the Treasury. "Treasury targets Hezbollah Fundraising network in the triple frontier of Argentina, Brazil, and Paraguay." Washington, DC, December 6, 2006

U.S. Government, U.S. Military, Department of Defense, U.S. Border Patrol. "Threat of Convergence of Terror Groups with Transnational Criminal Organizations to Utilize Existing Smuggling Routes and Techniques to Aid the Covert Entry of Operatives into the United States". Special Report. March 2017

U.S. Government, U.S. Military, Department of Defense. *Convergence: Illicit Networks and National Security in the Age of Globalization - Money Laundering, Threat Finance, Narcotics, Transnational Organized Crime, Sex Traffic, Black Market, Urbanization.* March 2017

VARGAS R, Humberto. "Bolivia: un País de Re-configuraciones por una Cultura de Pactos Políticos y de Conflictos." In *Movimientos Sociales y Conflicto en América Latina,* edited by Jose Seoanet, 85-102. Buenos Aires: CLACSO, 2003.

WERLAU Maria C. *Cuba's Intervention in Venezuela: A Strategic Occupation with Global Implications.* Miami: Neo Club Ediciones, 2019

www.ingramcontent.com/pod-product-compliance
Lightning Source LLC
Chambersburg PA
CBHW022106280326
41933CB00007B/278